JUST a MATTER of THYME

A Simple Collection of Satisfying Recipes

Recipes by Roxie Kelley and Friends

Illustrations by Shelly Reeves Smith

Andrews McMeel
Publishing, LLC
Kansas City

Shelly Reeves Smith and Roxie Kelley

Just a Matter of Thyme copyright © 2007 by Roxie Kelley. Illustrations © 2007 by Shelly Reeves Smith. All rights reserved. Printed in China. No part of this book may be used or reproduced in any manner whatsoever without written permission except in the case of reprints in the context of reviews. For information, write Andrews McMeel Publishing, LLC, an Andrews McMeel Universal company, 4520 Main Street, Kansas City, Missouri 64111.

08 09 10 11 WKT 10 9 8 7 6 5 4

ISBN-13: 978-0-7407-6534-6

ISBN-10: 0-7407-6534-5

Library of Congress Control Number: 2006938402

www.andrewsmcmeel.com

ATTENTION: SCHOOLS AND BUSINESSES

Andrews McMeel books are available at quantity discounts with bulk purchase for educational, business, or sales promotional use. For information, please write to: Special Sales Department, Andrews McMeel Publishing, LLC, 4520 Main Street, Kansas City, Missouri 64111.

Presented to :

I want a warm
and faithful friend,
To cheer the adverse hour ;
Who ne'er to flatter will descend,
Not bend the knee in power.
A friend to chide me when I'm wrong,
My inmost soul to see ;
That my friendship prove as strong
To him as his to me.

John Quincy Adams

A Note to our Friends

In order to write a cookbook that others will truly enjoy using, we believe that one must not only love good food, but love "gatherings" as well. You must enjoy other people loving good food.

A person who writes an unusually good cookbook feels that relationships are as necessary as nourishment, and that quality companionship makes an ordinary meal, a celebration.

Because you have chosen this book (or because someone thought enough about you to give you this book), we know something about you. You are a perceptive person. And you have perceived by now that this is not just another cookbook. It is a friendship book, a think-about-life-book... and because of Shelly's gifted hands, it is a literal work of art. We also know that it is "Just a Matter of Thyme" before you find pleasure and inspiration among these pages.

Thank you for allowing us to come into your home. We look forward to being a part of your gatherings.

Our best to you,
Roxie Kelley and
Shelly Reeves Smith

TABLE of CONTENTS

APPETIZERS

BREADS

(Breads, cont'd...)

SALADS and SALAD DRESSINGS

SOUPS

MAIN DISHES

ON'THE SIDE

CAKES and PIES

COOKIES and BROWNIES

" There is no love sincerer than the
love of food."

George Bernard Shaw

MISC.

Surround yourself with beauty today
And remind yourself of the gifts of each hour.
Sing out loud ~ even if the sound makes you laugh...
Love those around you deeply, and give of yourself to them,
then you will find that beauty
Not only surrounds you
but fills you...

Appetizers

" The ornaments of a
house are the guests
who frequent it . "

— Anonymous

Garden Party Fondue

2 - 8 oz. pkgs. Cream Cheese, softened
1 small onion, diced
¼ cup butter
¼ cup milk
¼ cup Parmesan Cheese
1 sm. pkg. dried beef, diced
Raw vegetables, chips, or crackers, for dipping

This recipe is prepared most easily in the microwave. Sauté the onion in melted butter until the onion bits are clear. Add the softened cream cheese, milk, Parmesan cheese, and dried beef and stir. Continue to heat and stir until smooth and warm. Serve warm with raw vegetables, chips or crackers.
Makes 8-10 servings.

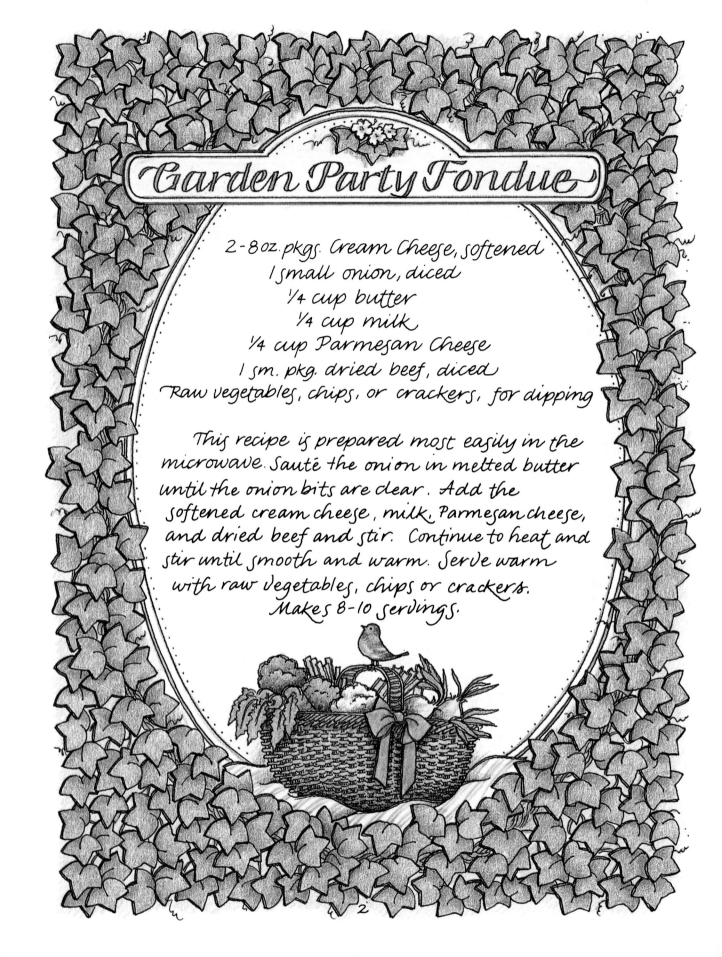

Kelly's
GOUDA·LOAF

2 wheels of Gouda Cheese, room temperature
1 pkg. of refrigerated crescent roll dough

Open packages of cheese and set aside.
Separate the crescent roll dough into two squares.
Lay the circle of cheese on the center of the
square and fold up the corners to meet at the
center of the top of the cheese. Moisten the
edges with a little bit of water to seal.
Repeat with the other circle of cheese and
dough. Lay each "loaf" on a cookie sheet a
few inches apart from each other. Bake at
350 degrees for about 15-20 minutes or
until golden brown. Allow to rest about
5 minutes before serving. Cut into wedges and...
Enjoy!

PEPPERCORN VEGETABLE Dip

2 cups real mayonnaise
¾ cup milk
¼ cup Parmesan cheese
1-2 Tbsp. freshly ground pepper
(It's more fun to use a blend of peppercorns if you have some on hand, but
just black peppercorns will do nicely.)
1 Tbsp. cider vinegar
1 tsp. lemon juice
1 tsp. minced onion
1 tsp. garlic salt
dash of Tabasco
dash of Worcestershire sauce

Wisk all ingredients until well
combined. Chill at least one hour
before serving.

Boursin Cheese Spread

½ cup butter, room temperature
2 8 oz. pkgs. cream cheese, softened
2 cloves garlic, crushed, or
   ½ tsp. garlic powder
½ tsp. oregano
¼ tsp. basil
¼ tsp. thyme
¼ tsp. marjoram
¼ tsp. dill weed
¼ tsp. freshly ground black pepper
A variety of crackers

Blend cream cheese and butter until smooth. Add seasonings and mix well. Chill overnight. Serve at room temperature with crackers.

AMIGO DIP

2 ripe avocados, peeled and cut into
    chunks
8 ounces cream cheese, softened
½ cup sour cream   2 Tbsp. milk
1 tsp. lemon juice   1½ tsp. chili powder

Blend all of the above ingredients in a
food processor or blender until creamy.
Spread this mixture on the bottom of a
large platter. Then layer the following
ingredients on top:

1 cup shredded head lettuce
2 tomatoes, diced   ⅔ cup diced gr. onion
1 cup shredded Cheddar or Jack cheese
1 jar of your favorite salsa (6-8 ounces)

Chill until ready to serve. Pass the
tortilla chips.

Note: This appetizer platter may also be
converted into individual "salads" for a
Mexican dinner. Try using small terra cotta
or ceramic dishes for each layered salad,
surrounding each with a circle of chips.
Garnish with a slice of lime, or a bit of fresh
cilantro if desired. Makes about 6 servings.

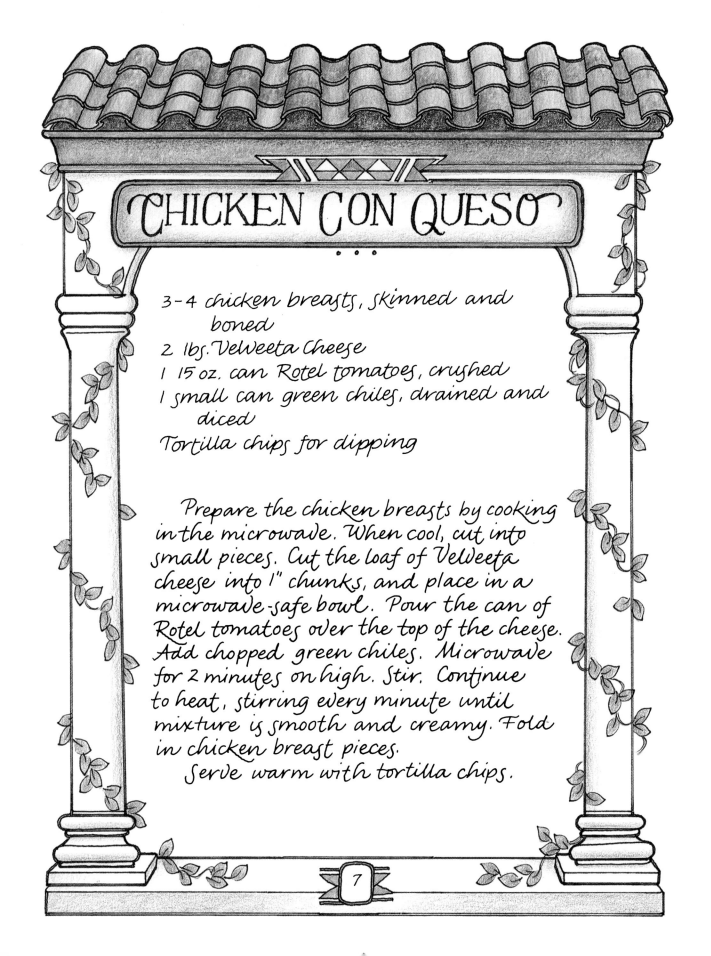

CHICKEN CON QUESO

3-4 chicken breasts, skinned and
    boned
2 lbs. Velveeta Cheese
1 15 oz. can Rotel tomatoes, crushed
1 small can green chiles, drained and
    diced
Tortilla chips for dipping

    Prepare the chicken breasts by cooking in the microwave. When cool, cut into small pieces. Cut the loaf of Velveeta cheese into 1" chunks, and place in a microwave-safe bowl. Pour the can of Rotel tomatoes over the top of the cheese. Add chopped green chiles. Microwave for 2 minutes on high. Stir. Continue to heat, stirring every minute until mixture is smooth and creamy. Fold in chicken breast pieces.
    Serve warm with tortilla chips.

PEOPLE seed

This is a cousin of "GORP" (good-old-raisins-and-peanuts), or a trail mix type snack. You may omit any ingredient listed below that does not appeal to you. Simply mix any or all of the ingredients below and store in a cool, dry place in an airtight container.

Raisins
Peanuts, cashews, almonds, etc.
M and M's
Chocolate Chips
Granola, or other cereal
dried fruits
coconut
pretzels
potato sticks
bagel chips

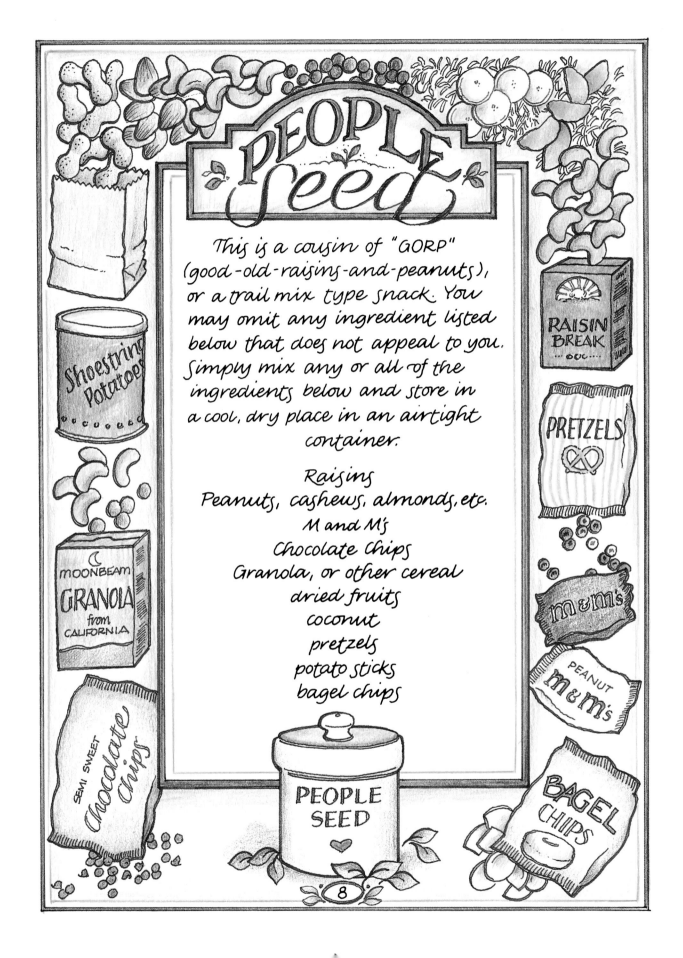

CRAB RANGOON

8 oz. crabmeat or
an imitation crabmeat
8 oz. cream cheese, softened
¼ tsp. garlic powder
¼ tsp. seasoned salt
16 oz. pkg. wonton wrappers
Vegetable oil for frying
water for moistening wonton skins
Sweet and Sour sauce or hot mustard sauce

Combine the crabmeat, cream cheese
and seasonings. Put ½ tsp. of the mixture in
the middle of each wonton skin. Fold points
of skin over to form a packet, sealing the
last point with a touch of water on your
fingertip. Deep fry until light golden brown.
Serve hot with sweet and sour
sauce or hot mustard sauce.

Makes about 4 dozen.

Chinese Chestnuts

2 5oz. cans whole water
~chestnuts, drained
¼ cup sugar
1 Tbsp. brown sugar
¼ tsp. ginger
½ cup soy sauce
15 strips bacon
toothpicks

Mix sugars, ginger and soy sauce.
Cut chestnuts in half. Soak chestnuts in
mixture for about 30 minutes. Cut bacon
in half and wrap each chestnut with
a piece of bacon. Secure with a toothpick.* Bake at 375° for 15 - 20 minutes in a baking dish or pan.
Serve hot. Makes about 30.

* May be refrigerated at this point
up to one day, and baked later.

COCKTAIL PIZZAS

1 lb. pork sausage
3 Tbsp. Worcestershire
2 (5 oz.) jars Kraft Old English cheese spread
¼ cup catsup
¼ tsp. oregano
2 loaves "party" or miniature rye bread

Brown the sausage and drain. Add Worcestershire, cheese spread, catsup, and oregano. Stir on medium-low heat until mixed well. Remove from heat and spread about 1 Tbsp. of mixture onto each slice of miniature rye bread. Place on foil-lined cookie sheet and bake at 400° for 10 minutes. Serve hot.

Serves 8-10.

11

Love

" Love is the only flower
that grows and blossoms
without the aid of seasons . "
~ Kahlil Gibran

" The best smell is bread,
the best saver salt , the best love
that of children . "
~ George Herbert

" That best portion of a good man's life,
His little , nameless, unremembered acts
of kindness and of love."
~ William Wordsworth

"If you would be loved, love and be loveable. "
~ Benjamin Franklin

" Traveling in the company of
those we love is home in motion."
~ Leigh Hunt

Banana Nut Muffins

2 cups flour
1 Tbsp. baking powder
½ tsp. salt
½ cup butter
1 cup sugar
2 eggs
1⅓ cups mashed, ripe bananas

1 cup chopped pecans or walnuts

Sift together flour, baking powder and salt. Set aside. Cream together butter and sugar. Beat in eggs, one at a time. Stir in mashed bananas. Add dry ingredients all at once, stirring just enough to moisten. Gently stir in nuts. Spoon into greased muffin tin, filling ⅔ full. Bake in 350° oven for 18-20 minutes or until golden. Makes 15-18 muffins.

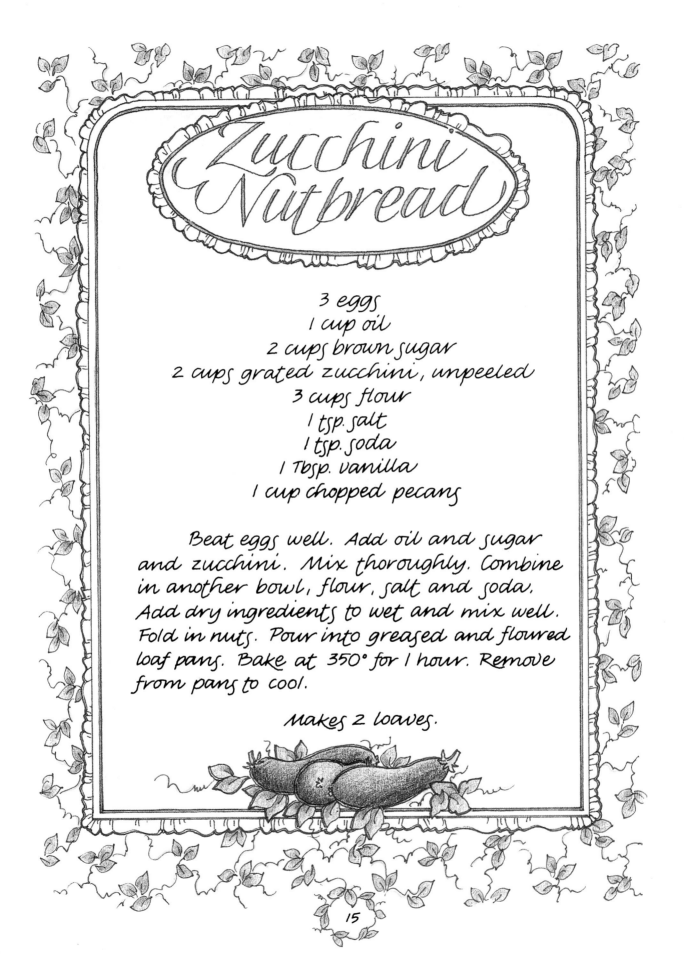

Zucchini Nutbread

3 eggs
1 cup oil
2 cups brown sugar
2 cups grated zucchini, unpeeled
3 cups flour
1 tsp. salt
1 tsp. soda
1 Tbsp. vanilla
1 cup chopped pecans

Beat eggs well. Add oil and sugar and zucchini. Mix thoroughly. Combine in another bowl, flour, salt and soda. Add dry ingredients to wet and mix well. Fold in nuts. Pour into greased and floured loaf pans. Bake at 350° for 1 hour. Remove from pans to cool.

Makes 2 loaves.

Banana ~ Carrot
N U T B R E A D

2 cups flour
1 tsp. baking soda
½ tsp. salt
½ tsp. cinnamon
1 cup mashed, ripe bananas
1 cup sugar
3/4 cup vegetable oil
2 eggs
1 cup finely grated, pared carrots
½ cup chopped pecans

Sift together flour baking soda,
salt and cinnamon. Set aside. Combine
bananas, sugar, oil and eggs. Beat with
electric mixer at medium speed for
2 minutes. Stir in dry ingredients. Fold
in carrots and pecans. Spread in
greased and floured loaf pan.
(Use the largest loaf pan you
have available.) Bake in 350°
oven 55 minutes or until
wooden toothpick comes
out clean.

Fresh Peach Muffins

1 egg
1 cup milk
¼ cup butter, melted
⅔ cup sugar
½ tsp. salt
¼ tsp. cinnamon
1 tsp. lemon juice
¼ tsp. vanilla
2 cups flour
1 Tbsp. baking powder
1 cup diced, peeled peaches

Beat egg. Stir in next seven ingredients. In a separate bowl, mix together flour and baking powder. Add to milk mixture and stir just until blended. Do not overmix.

Fold in peaches. Grease muffin tins and fill ⅔ full. Makes about one dozen. Bake at 400° for 18-20 minutes.

Blueberry Peach Cinnamon

MUFFINS

½ cup blueberries
½ cup peaches, peeled
  and diced
3 cups flour
½ cup sugar
½ cup brown sugar
1 Tbsp. baking powder
1 tsp. salt
½ cup butter, melted
3 eggs, beaten
1 cup milk
4 Tbsp. butter, melted
2 Tbsp. sugar and
2 tsp. cinnamon, mixed

Mix flour, sugars, baking powder, and salt. Add butter, beaten eggs and milk, stirring just until blended. Carefully fold in fruit. Fill greased muffin cups about ⅔ full. Bake at 400° for 18-20 minutes, or until golden.

Brush tops with melted butter and sprinkle with cinnamon-sugar mixture.

Enjoy!

Makes about 1 dozen.

Whole Wheat Pecan Waffles

1 ¾ cup whole wheat flour
1 tsp. salt
1 Tbsp. baking powder
½ cup chopped pecans

Stir the above ingredients together. Set aside.
In a separate bowl combine:

1 ¾ cup milk
½ cup vegetable oil
2 eggs, beaten

Stir egg mixture into flour mixture just
until moistened. Grease waffle iron. Pour batter
on hot waffle iron. Bake. Pass the butter, powdered
sugar, honey and/or syrup.
Serves 2-4.

BEEF & CHEDDAR Bread

3 cups flour
(I use half white and half wheat)

1 pkg. dry yeast
1 Tbsp. minced onion
1 tsp. salt
¼ cup water
2 cups grated Cheddar
   cheese

2 Tbsp. sugar
1 egg, separated
1 cup milk
2 Tbsp. butter
1 small package
   dried beef, diced

Heat milk, water, and butter until warm. Mix 2 cups of the flour, yeast, sugar, onion, and salt in a medium-sized mixing bowl. Pour liquid mixture over dry mixture. Add beaten egg yolk, mix well for 3 minutes. Stir in remaining flour by hand. Spread evenly in a greased 10" x 15" pan. At this point you may want to beat the egg white slightly and dip your finger tips in it as you spread the dough in the pan. It will make the spreading a little easier if the dough is sticky. Use the remaining egg white to brush evenly over the surface of the dough. Sprinkle with cheese and beef. Bake at 375° for 20-25 minutes until golden brown.

Serves 8-10.

MacIntosh Muffins

1¼ cup vegetable oil
2 cups sugar
3 cups flour
3 eggs
2 tsp. vanilla
1 tsp. baking soda
1 tsp. cinnamon
1 tsp. salt
2 cups MacIntosh apples, chopped and peeled
(you may substitute with other types of
baking apples)
1 cup chopped pecans
1 cup coconut

Mix all ingredients together until well-
blended. Fill greased muffin tins about 2/3
full. Makes about 2-3 dozen. Bake in
350° oven for about 25 minutes or
until golden brown. These muffins
will not have much of a "crown"
on top. They are very dense
in texture.

Pumpkin Muffins

1⅓ cups sugar   ½ cup butter
2 eggs   2 cups flour
4 tsp. baking powder   1 tsp. cinnamon
½ tsp. salt   1 cup pumpkin
4 Tbsp. milk

Cream together sugar and butter.
Add eggs and beat well. In a separate bowl, combine flour, baking powder, cinnamon, and salt. In yet another bowl, combine pumpkin and milk. Add flour mixture and pumpkin mixture alternately to creamed mixture, beating well after each addition. Spoon into greased muffin tins (makes about 2 dozen).
Bake at 350° for 18 - 20 minutes.

Pumpkin Nutbread

3⅓ cups flour
4 tsp. pumpkin pie spice
2 tsp. baking soda
1 tsp. baking powder
1½ tsp. salt
2⅔ cup sugar
⅔ cup oil
4 eggs
1 lb. can mashed pumpkin
⅔ cup water
½ cup chopped pecans, optional

Sift together flour, pumpkin pie spice, soda, powder, and salt. Set aside. Beat together sugar and oil until light. Add eggs, one at a time. Beat in pumpkin. Add dry ingredients alternately with water to sugar mixture. Stir in pecans. Pour into 2 greased 9" x 5" x 3" loaf pans. Bake in 325° oven for 55-60 minutes or until tester comes out clean when inserted into center of the loaf.
Freezes well.

2 cups quick-cooking oatmeal
2 cups buttermilk
2 eggs
²/₃ cup oil
1 cup brown sugar
2 cups flour
1 tsp. salt
1 tsp. soda
2 tsp. baking powder

Mix the first two ingredients together and let stand 45-60 minutes.
Add eggs and oil to oatmeal mixture.
Mix remaining ingredients together in a separate bowl. Add liquid ingredients, mixing well. Pour into greased muffin tins. Makes about 24.
Bake in a 400° oven 15-20 minutes or until golden brown.

with natural oat bran

GOOD & Good for you!

ALL BRAN BREAD

1 cup butter	Mix and cool
3/4 cup sugar	until just
1½ tsp. salt	warm.
1 cup boiling water	
1½ cup All Bran	
2 pkgs. yeast	Dissolve yeast
1 cup warm water	in water and add to above.
2 eggs, beaten	Add to above
3 cups flour	and blend well.
3-4 cups flour	Add gradually to above, kneading until smooth and elastic.

Put into a greased bowl. Turn greased side up. Cover lightly with plastic wrap and let rise in a warm place until doubled (about 1 hour). Punch down and let rise 10 minutes. Divide dough into two equal parts and shape into loaves. Place each into a greased loaf pan. Cover and let rise an additional 30-40 minutes. Bake in a 375° oven for about 40-50 minutes or until golden.

Bran Muffins

1¼ cup flour

¼ tsp. salt

1½ cup bran cereal

1 egg, beaten

1 Tbsp. baking powder

½ cup sugar

1¼ cup milk

¼ cup vegetable oil

Combine cereal and milk in a large bowl and let stand for 2 minutes. Combine dry ingredients in a separate bowl. Add egg and oil to cereal mixture and beat well. Add dry ingredients all at once, stirring only until combined. Spoon into greased muffin cups and bake at 400° for 15-17 minutes. Makes about 1 dozen. This batter may be refrigerated for up to two weeks before baking.

FARMHOUSE CHEDDAR
· M U F F I N S ·

2 cups flour
1 Tbsp. baking powder
1 tsp. salt
½ tsp. paprika
2 Tbsp. sugar
1 egg, beaten
½ cup milk
½ cup sour cream
⅓ cup butter, melted
1 cup Cheddar cheese, shredded
½ cup chopped onion, sautéed in 2 Tbsp. butter
¼ cup fresh parsley or 1-2 tsp. dill weed

Stir together flour, baking powder, salt, paprika, and sugar. Add egg, milk, sour cream, butter and cheese. Stir just until blended. Fold in onions and parsley. Bake at 400° in greased muffin tin for about 20 minutes or until golden. Makes about 1 dozen.

Italian
CHEESE TOPPED BREAD

1 loaf French bread, split in half lengthwise
6 Tbsp. butter
½ cup grated Romano cheese
½ cup grated Parmesan Cheese
6 oz. sliced Mozzarella
¼ tsp. garlic powder
1 Tbsp. parsley flakes

Melt butter and add Romano and Parmesan cheeses, parsley and garlic powder. Cover cut surface of bread with Mozzarella cheese. Spread butter mixture over the Mozzarella slices. Bake on cookie sheet at 375° for about 10-15 minutes, or until cheese is bubbly and edges of bread are toasty. Cut into slices and serve hot.

Serves 6-8.

Dilly Cheese
B·R·E·A·D

3 cups biscuit mix
1½ cups grated Cheddar cheese
1 Tbsp. sugar
1¼ cups milk
1 egg, beaten
1 Tbsp. vegetable oil
½ tsp. Dill
½ tsp. dry mustard

Combine biscuit mix, cheese and sugar in a large bowl. Combine remaining ingredients in a second bowl and mix well. Stir into dry mixture, blending thoroughly. Then beat slightly to remove lumps. Turn into a greased 5 x 9" loaf pan and bake until golden brown at 350° for about 45-50 minutes.
Serves 6-8.

Sweet Corn Bread

4 tsp. salt
4½ cups flour
3½ cups yellow cornmeal
1½ cups non-fat dry milk
¼ cup baking powder
1⅓ cup brown sugar
1¾ cups white vegetable shortening

Mix all dry ingredients in a large bowl. Work in shortening until evenly distributed. Transfer to an airtight container and store in a cool dry place. This mix will keep well for 3 months and will make 3 recipes (about 1 dozen muffins per recipe). The mix will be crumbly, not smooth in texture!

To prepare one recipe of muffins, you will need:

2 eggs   1⅓ cups water
4½ cups of mix

Break the eggs into the water and beat slightly. Add to dry mix and stir just enough to blend. Using a ⅓ cup measuring cup, scoop batter into a greased 12-cup muffin tin. Bake at 425° for 15-20 minutes or until golden brown.

MIX

English Muffin BREAD

This is a wonderful recipe for those who have been searching for a low-sugar and low-fat bread. When I opened the bakery in our town several years ago, one of my favorite mother-daughter friendships came to my rescue with this recipe. A special thanks to Mary and Paula for their willingness to share what became one of the most popular breads we prepared.

3 pkgs. rapid rise yeast
7-8 cups white flour
2 cups wheat flour
¼ cup sugar
1 Tbsp. salt
3 cups warm water
corn meal for the bottom of the pan

Mix yeast, 2 cups white flour, 2 cups wheat flour, sugar and salt. Pour warm water over all and mix well for 3 minutes. Keep adding additional white flour kneading until smooth and elastic. This will take about 10-15 minutes. Divide into 3 parts. Place in a greased and corn meal-coated loaf pan. Cover loosely with plastic wrap and place in a warm place to rise until doubled (about 30-45 minutes). Gently pull the plastic wrap off and bake about 30-40 minutes in a 350° oven.

Light Wheat Rolls

This is such a versatile recipe!
Once you become familiar with it, you will want
to try making the Ham and Cheddar Rolls and
the Missouri Morning Cinnamon Rolls that use this
dough as a starting point.

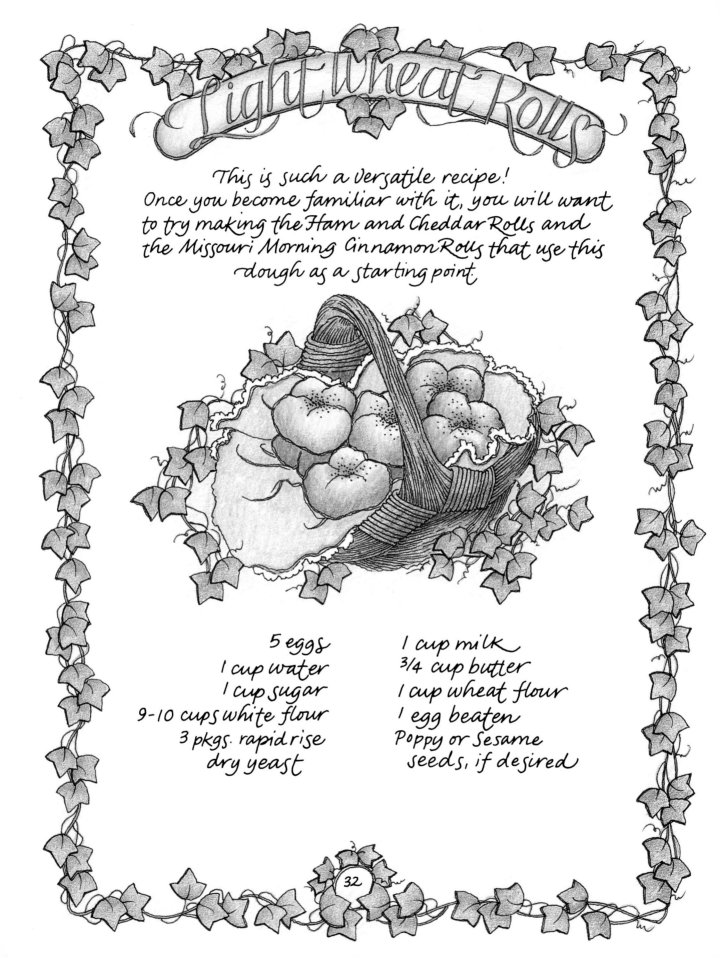

5 eggs
1 cup water
1 cup sugar
9-10 cups white flour
3 pkgs. rapid rise
dry yeast

1 cup milk
3/4 cup butter
1 cup wheat flour
1 egg beaten
Poppy or Sesame
seeds, if desired

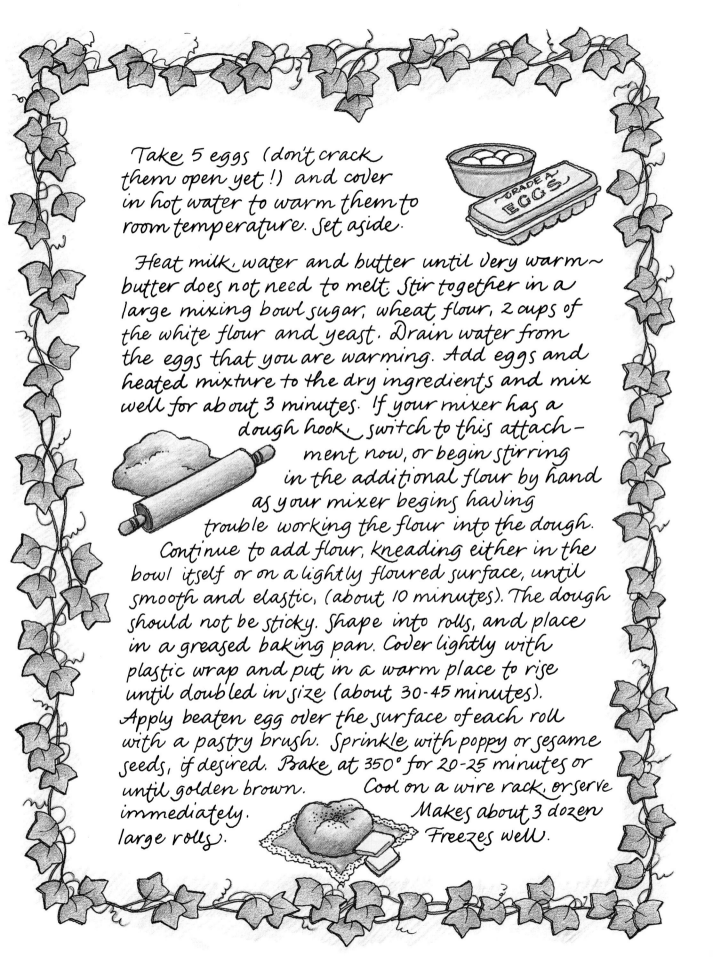

Take 5 eggs (don't crack them open yet!) and cover in hot water to warm them to room temperature. Set aside.

Heat milk, water and butter until very warm~ butter does not need to melt. Stir together in a large mixing bowl sugar, wheat, flour, 2 cups of the white flour and yeast. Drain water from the eggs that you are warming. Add eggs and heated mixture to the dry ingredients and mix well for about 3 minutes. If your mixer has a dough hook, switch to this attach- ment now, or begin stirring in the additional flour by hand as your mixer begins having trouble working the flour into the dough. Continue to add flour, kneading either in the bowl itself or on a lightly floured surface, until smooth and elastic, (about 10 minutes). The dough should not be sticky. Shape into rolls, and place in a greased baking pan. Cover lightly with plastic wrap and put in a warm place to rise until doubled in size (about 30-45 minutes). Apply beaten egg over the surface of each roll with a pastry brush. Sprinkle with poppy or sesame seeds, if desired. Bake at 350° for 20-25 minutes or until golden brown. Cool on a wire rack, or serve immediately. Makes about 3 dozen large rolls. Freezes well.

Missouri Morning Cinnamon Rolls

3-4 Tbsp. cinnamon
2-3 cups sugar
1 cup butter, softened

> Mix together...

2 cups powdered sugar and 2-3 Tbsp. water
Mix until smooth for icing.

Prepare the Light Wheat Roll Recipe to the shaping point. Divide the dough into two equal parts. Roll out one part on a lightly floured surface into an 18"x 13" rectangle. Spread generously with half of butter. Sprinkle with half of the cinnamon-sugar mixture. Starting at short end, roll up tightly (but without "stretching the dough too thin") into a log. Using a dough scraper or a large knife, cut into 1½" slices and place spiral side up in a greased baking dish. To allow for rising, make sure there is about ½" between each roll so that they won't be too crowded. Repeat with other half of dough. Cover lightly with plastic wrap and let rise in a warm place for about 30-40 minutes, or until doubled. Bake in 350° oven for 25-28 minutes or until golden brown. Drizzle warm rolls with powdered sugar icing. Makes about 2 dozen rolls.

Cream Cheese Danish

1 Recipe
Missouri Morning Cinnamon Rolls

8 ounces cream cheese, softened
6 Tbsp. sugar
1 egg
½ tsp. vanilla
1½ cup chopped pecans

2 cups powdered sugar
and
2-3 Tbsp. water
Mix until smooth and
reserve for icing after
baking.

Slice cinnamon roll dough into 1" pieces and place in a greased muffin tin. Cover lightly with plastic wrap and let rise 30-40 minutes. Meanwhile, prepare topping by mixing cream cheese, sugar, egg and vanilla until smooth. When rolls are done rising, top each with about a tablespoon of cream cheese mixture and sprinkle with pecans. Bake in a 350° oven for about 20-25 minutes. Remove from pan and drizzle with powdered sugar icing.
Makes 2-3 dozen.

HAM & CHEDDAR Rolls

1# Ham, sliced thin
1# Cheddar cheese,
(sliced very thin or shredded)
1 cup butter softened
4-5 green onion tops, sliced
1 egg, beaten

Prepare

the Light Wheat Roll Recipe to the shaping stage. Divide the dough into two equal parts. Roll out one part on a lightly floured surface into an 18" x 13" rectangle. Spread with half of butter. Arrange half of ham slices over the top of the dough and repeat with cheese. Sprinkle with half of the green onion tops. Starting at the short end, roll up tightly into a log. Cut into 1" slices.

Place each piece into a greased muffin cup, squeezing slightly, so that the center of the roll is a little higher in the pan than the sides of the roll. Repeat with other half of dough. Cover muffin tins lightly with plastic wrap and let rise until doubled (about 30-40 minutes). Brush the rolls with beaten egg. Bake at 350° for about 20-24 minutes or until golden brown.

Makes about 3 dozen.

Note

All three of these recipes ~ the Light Wheat Rolls, the Cinnamon Rolls, and the Ham and Cheddar Rolls ~ may be refrigerated after shaping (and before rising) for up to 18 hours. Take out of the refrigerator when you wish 1½ hours before you wish to serve them. Let rise in a warm place for about one hour. Brush with beaten egg, if recipe requires. Bake according to the directions.

Enjoy!

Children

"Dear Lord, I do not ask
that thou shouldst give me
some high work of thine
some noble calling, or some wonderous task.
Give me a little hand to hold in mine.
Give me a little child to point the way
over the strange, sweet path that leads to thee.
Give me a little voice to teach to pray.
Give me two shining eyes thy face to see.
The only crown I ask, Dear Lord, to wear is this,
that I may teach a little child.
I do not ask that I may ever stand
among the wise, the worthy, or the great
I only ask that softly hand-in-hand,
a child and I may enter at the gate."

~ Anonymous

"Keep me away from the wisdom
which does not cry,
the philosophy which does not laugh,
and the greatness which does not
bow before children."

~ Kahlil Gibran

Salads

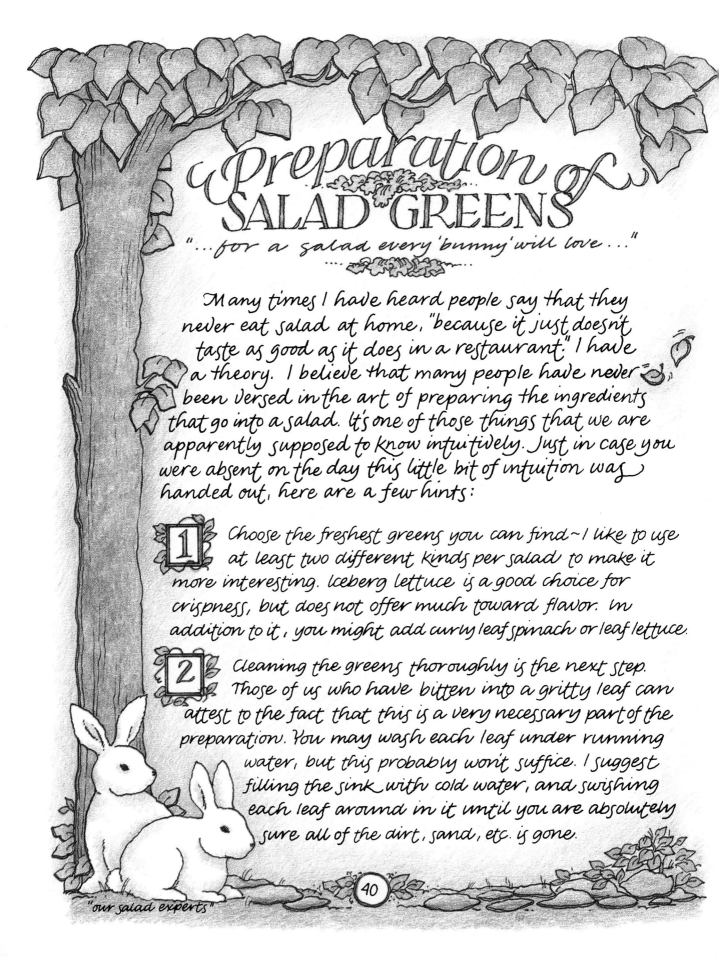

Preparation of SALAD GREENS

"...for a salad every 'bunny' will love..."

Many times I have heard people say that they never eat salad at home, "because it just doesn't taste as good as it does in a restaurant." I have a theory. I believe that many people have never been versed in the art of preparing the ingredients that go into a salad. It's one of those things that we are apparently supposed to know intuitively. Just in case you were absent on the day this little bit of intuition was handed out, here are a few hints:

1 Choose the freshest greens you can find ~ I like to use at least two different kinds per salad to make it more interesting. Iceberg lettuce is a good choice for crispness, but does not offer much toward flavor. In addition to it, you might add curly leaf spinach or leaf lettuce.

2 Cleaning the greens thoroughly is the next step. Those of us who have bitten into a gritty leaf can attest to the fact that this is a very necessary part of the preparation. You may wash each leaf under running water, but this probably won't suffice. I suggest filling the sink with cold water, and swishing each leaf around in it until you are absolutely sure all of the dirt, sand, etc. is gone.

"our salad experts"

3 Once you are sure that the greens are sparkling clean, the next step is to make sure that each leaf is dry. You may shake off the extra moisture and dab each piece with paper towels. But they are probably still not dry enough. At this point, you may use a salad spinner to throw off extra moisture. But my favorite and most economical device for this job is a pillowcase. That's right. A pillowcase. Make sure that it is clean and that there are no "fuzz bunnies" in the corners. Place the greens in the pillowcase. Go outside. Gather up the open end in your hand. Make sure you are a safe distance away from anyone or anything that you don't want to "shower". Now swing the pillowcase around and around in the air to "throw out" any extra moisture left on the greens.

a "gourmet pillowcase"

4 Go back inside. Remove the greens from the pillowcase and lay out on dry paper towels. Cover with another layer of paper towels, and store in a plastic bag or covered container for up to 4-5 days, or until use.

You've probably concluded by now that one of the best kept secrets to a good salad is to start with very clean and very dry greens. Both of these qualities are important and should not be overlooked. Now, use your new-found expertise to prepare any of the salads in this book or any of your past favorites.

a "fuzz bunny"

How To Boil An Egg

It always amazes me how many people are truly impressed with this technique. I suppose it is because we have all had the nerve-racking experience of "the egg that refused to peel". Try this technique the next time you need a hard cooked egg:

1 Place eggs in a saucepan. Cover with cold water.

2  Bring to a rapid boil. Immediately place the lid on the pan.

3 Leave the pan on the burner, but turn the burner off. Let set for 15 minutes.

4 Drain off hot water. Cover cooked eggs again with cold water. Let set 2 minutes.

5 Drain off cold water. Leaving the eggs in the pan, shake pan back and forth several times, so that the eggs bump up against each other and crack. The shell should slide off easily now. Rinse under cool water and store in a covered container or plastic bag until use. Use within 3 days.

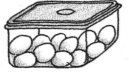

BITS & PIECES SALAD

1 head of iceberg lettuce
(See "Preparation of Salad Greens")

1 head of leaf lettuce
or spinach

1 cup frozen
peas, (thawed)

2 eggs, hard-boiled
(See "How to Boil an Egg")

¼ cup sunflower nuts

1 or 2 ounces
alfalfa sprouts

1 cup
shredded
Cheddar
cheese

Prepare salad greens
and toss with the
remaining ingredients. Pass the dressing
and croutons, and…

Enjoy!

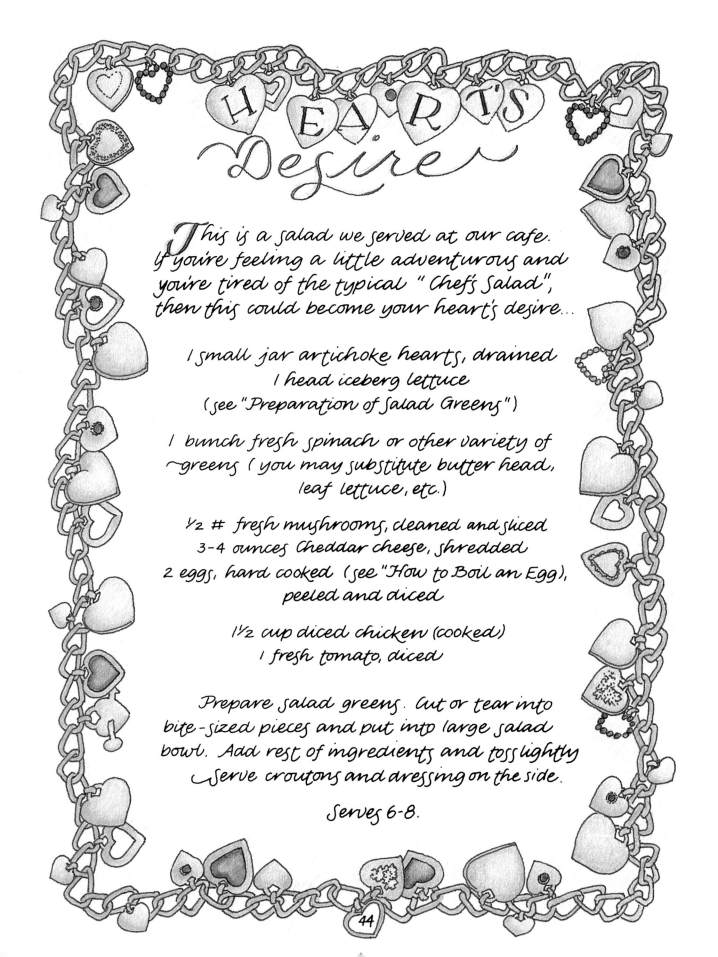

HEARTS Desire

This is a salad we served at our cafe. If you're feeling a little adventurous and you're tired of the typical "Chef's Salad", then this could become your heart's desire...

1 small jar artichoke hearts, drained
1 head iceberg lettuce
(see "Preparation of Salad Greens")

1 bunch fresh spinach or other variety of greens (you may substitute butter head, leaf lettuce, etc.)

½ # fresh mushrooms, cleaned and sliced
3-4 ounces Cheddar cheese, shredded
2 eggs, hard cooked (see "How to Boil an Egg), peeled and diced

1½ cup diced chicken (cooked)
1 fresh tomato, diced

Prepare salad greens. Cut or tear into bite-sized pieces and put into large salad bowl. Add rest of ingredients and toss lightly. Serve croutons and dressing on the side.

Serves 6-8.

CAPITOLA'S COLE SLAW

1 medium head of cabbage, shredded
1 carrot, peeled and shredded
¼ cup sugar
½ cup mayonnaise
¼ cup vinegar
celery seed, salt and pepper
to taste

Combine all of the above ingredients
and store in a covered container in the refrigerator. Best when made the day before.

Serves 6-8.

MY GRANDMA'S POTATO SALAD

8 medium sized potatoes
6 eggs, hard-boiled (see "How to Boil an Egg")
½ lb. bacon (optional)
1 rib celery, diced
¼ cup mayonnaise
¼ cup sour cream
1 Tbsp. sugar
¼ cup sweet pickle relish
2 Tbsp. chives
2-3 Tbsp. prepared mustard
salt and pepper to taste

Place potatoes in a good sized pot. Cover with water. Bring to a boil and cook until just tender. Drain off hot water. Allow potatoes to cool. Then peel and cut into chunks. Prepare eggs. Peel and dice, and add to the potatoes. Fry bacon until crisp. Crumble into potato and egg mixture. Add celery pieces. Gently fold in the remaining ingredients until well-blended. Store in the refrigerator in a covered container until use.
Serves 10-12.

Fried CHICKEN SALAD

1 head iceberg lettuce and 1 bunch leaf lettuce
(see "Preparation of Salad Greens")
1 carrot, peeled and cut into Julienne strips
2 eggs, peeled and diced
(see "How to Boil an Egg")

1 tomato, diced
½ # bacon, cooked until crisp~
then cut into small pieces

3-4 chicken breasts, cut into bite-sized pieces
1 cup milk
seasoned salt
freshly ground pepper
2 cups flour
vegetable oil for frying

Let chicken pieces sit in milk. Mix salt and pepper with flour. Set aside. Meanwhile, prepare eggs and bacon. Set aside. Prepare salad greens. Tear or cut into bite-sized pieces and put into large salad bowl. Add carrots and set in the refrigerator while you prepare the chicken.

Dip each piece of chicken into the flour mixture and carefully place into hot oil. Fry until golden brown and tender. This should only take 2-3 minutes per batch. Be careful not to crowd chicken while frying. Drain on paper towels. Remove salad from the refrigerator. Add tomato, bacon, eggs and chicken. Pass the croutons and salad dressing. Serves 6-8.

Italian Salad

1 head iceberg lettuce
and 1 head Romaine
1 small jar sliced pimento
1 can Hearts of Palm, drained and sliced
1 jar Artichoke Hearts, drained and cut in halves
1 purple onion, sliced
1 cup Provel cheese, shredded
¼ lb. hard salami, sliced and diced (optional)
Parmesan cheese, grated
Fresh ground pepper to taste
your favorite vinegar and oil dressing

See "Preparation of Salad Greens". After washing
and drying lettuces, tear into small pieces and place
in a large salad bowl. Add all other ingredients
with the exception of the dressing. Keep refrigerated
until serving time. Toss with dressing just before
serving. Serves about 6.

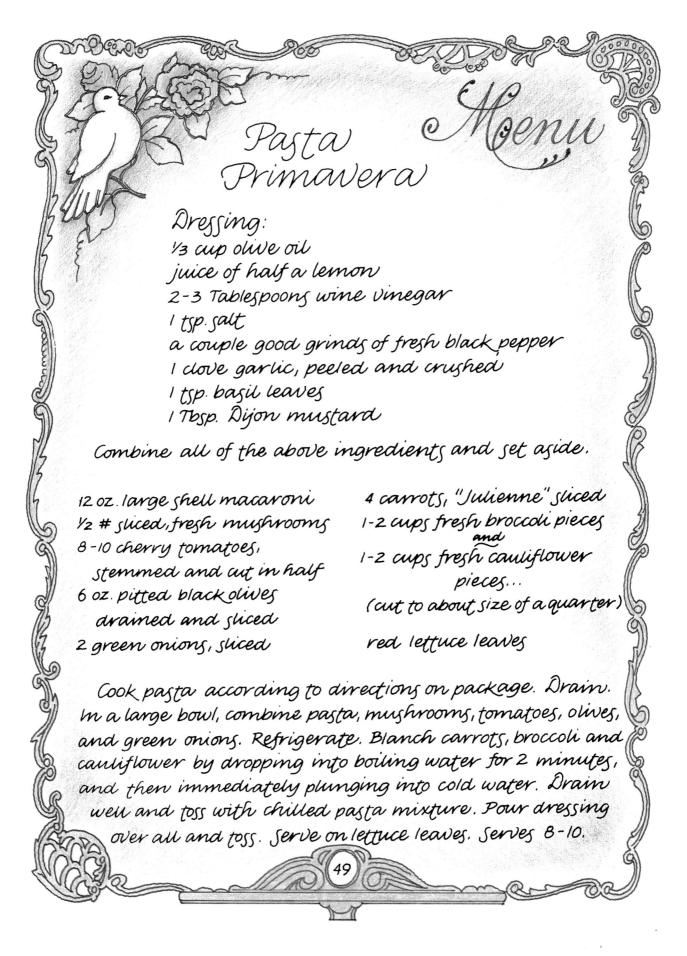

Pasta Primavera

Dressing:

⅓ cup olive oil

juice of half a lemon

2-3 Tablespoons wine vinegar

1 tsp. salt

a couple good grinds of fresh black pepper

1 clove garlic, peeled and crushed

1 tsp. basil leaves

1 Tbsp. Dijon mustard

Combine all of the above ingredients and set aside.

12 oz. large shell macaroni

½ # sliced, fresh mushrooms

8-10 cherry tomatoes, stemmed and cut in half

6 oz. pitted black olives drained and sliced

2 green onions, sliced

4 carrots, "Julienne" sliced

1-2 cups fresh broccoli pieces

and

1-2 cups fresh cauliflower pieces...

(cut to about size of a quarter)

red lettuce leaves

Cook pasta according to directions on package. Drain. In a large bowl, combine pasta, mushrooms, tomatoes, olives, and green onions. Refrigerate. Blanch carrots, broccoli and cauliflower by dropping into boiling water for 2 minutes, and then immediately plunging into cold water. Drain well and toss with chilled pasta mixture. Pour dressing over all and toss. Serve on lettuce leaves. Serves 8-10.

CHERRY PIE Jell-o Salad

Prepare
one large package of
cherry Jell-O using half as
much cold water as directed.
Add one can of cherry pie filling that
has been mixed with 1 Tablespoon of sugar.

Chill until set.

Mix 4 ounces of cream cheese and
8 ounces of whipped topping until smooth
(Hint: cream cheese should be at room temperature).

Fold in a small can of crushed
pineapple that has been well-drained.
Spread on top of set Jell-O.
Sprinkle with pecans.

Serves about 8.

MOUNTAIN SPRING
fruit salad

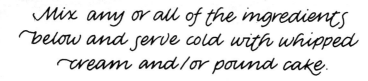

Mix any or all of the ingredients below and serve cold with whipped cream and/or pound cake.

½ cup apple chunks
1 cup pineapple chunks
(if not using fresh pineapple, please drain off the juice of the canned pineapple before adding to the salad.)

½ cup mandarin,
or fresh, peeled orange slices

1 cup sliced peaches, fresh or frozen
1 cup strawberries, fresh or frozen
2 bananas, sliced
¼ cup pecan pieces
2-3 Tablespoons, sugar to taste

Hint:
Add bananas at the last minute.
Serves about 6.

Orange Raspberry Garden Salad

1 bunch fresh spinach
(See "Preparation of Salad Greens")
1 head of Boston Bib lettuce, or Romaine
1 small can of Mandarin oranges, drained
or 2 fresh oranges (peeled and diced)
½ cup sliced almonds

Toss above ingredients together and add
dressing just before serving.

Dressing

Wisk together or shake in a jar:

⅓ cup vegetable oil
⅓ cup fresh orange juice
3 Tbsp. raspberry vinegar
(Red wine vinegar may be substituted here if you
have trouble locating raspberry vinegar
in your local store.)
1 Tbsp. sugar
salt and freshly ground pepper to taste
1 clove garlic, peeled and crushed

CHICKEN · SALAD

3 whole chicken breasts,
  skinned and boned
seasoned salt
~poultry seasoning
freshly ground pepper
~vegetable oil pan coating
½ cup real mayonnaise

1 rib celery, diced
1 cup white seedless grapes,
  cut in half
½ cup sweet pickle relish
3 eggs, hard cooked,
  (then peeled and diced)
1 tsp. of your favorite
  prepared mustard

Sauté chicken breasts in a   pan sprayed with vegetable coating. Season to your taste with the salt, poultry seasoning, and pepper. Brown lightly on both sides, cooking until tender, but not dry. Set aside until cool enough to dice. Mix with the remaining ingredients and refrigerate until serving. This may be served as a sandwich with lettuce and tomato, or on top of a bed of lettuce as a salad.

Serves 4-6.

THE WELL-DRESSED SALAD

RANCH STYLE DRESSING MIX

5 Tbsp. instant minced onion
4 tsp. salt
1 tsp. garlic powder
7 Tbsp. parsley flakes

Mix all together and store in a cool, dry, place in a covered container. To prepare, combine 2 Tbsp. of the mix with 1 cup mayonnaise and 1 cup buttermilk. Sour cream may be substituted for the buttermilk to make a vegetable or chip dip.

PEPPERCREAM DRESSING

If you will look under "Peppercorn Vegetable Dip" in the appetizer section, you will find this recipe. You may find that it is a little easier to pour as a dressing if you add a few more tablespoons of milk than is called for in the dip recipe. Peppercream Dressing is from the kitchen of Mike Atwell, a wonderful gourmet cook from our resort area. Thanks, Mike!

This recipe will always be one of my favorites because it brings back memories of the two wonderful years I spent in the home of Rev. and Mrs. Clyde Chiles. Mrs. Chiles taught me how to love and appreciate all types of foods. But more importantly, she instilled in me a lifelong hunger for "spiritual foods" as well... There were always several choices of fresh vegetables at every meal and a dinner salad accompanied by this dressing:

Mrs. Chiles'
SWEET 'N' SOUR
Italian Dressing

1 cup sugar
1½ cups vinegar
2 packets Good Seasons Italian Dressing Mix
2 ice cubes
¼ cup vegetable oil

Bring vinegar to a boil. Remove from heat. Add sugar and stir until dissolved. Add dressing mix, then ice. Stir until the ice melts, then add oil. Store in a covered container in the refrigerator. Shake well before serving.

Home

"The happiest moments in my life
have been the few that I passed
at home in the bosom of my family."

~ Thomas Jefferson

" The beauty of the house is order,
The blessing of the house is contentment;
The glory of the house is hospitality."

~ House Blessing

" Always I have a chair for you
in the smallest parlor in the world,
to wit, my heart."

~ Emily Dickinson

Peace be within thy walls,
and prosperity within thy palaces.

~ Psalms 122:7

Soups

GOOSE SOUP

There is no goose in this soup...
However it is a specialty of one of our dearest friends
and co-workers, whose nickname is "Goose". Joyce is
also known around the office as "the woman who can
do anything". If she were serving this soup to you
today, it would be garnished with fresh tarragon
from her garden.

8 oz. fresh mushrooms, sliced
1 medium leek onion, sliced
½ cup butter
½ cup flour
2 (14½ oz.) cans chicken broth
1 can artichoke hearts, drained and quartered
1 tsp. tarragon
½ tsp. salt
fresh ground pepper
2 tsp. fresh lemon juice
few drops tobasco sauce
½ pint whipping cream

Sauté mushrooms and onion in butter in a dutch oven
over medium heat until tender. Add flour, stirring until
smooth. Slowly add chicken broth, stirring constantly. Add
next six ingredients. Simmer until slightly thickened.
Add cream and heat slowly until warm. Serves 4.

Goose

COLONIAL VEGETABLE Soup

3 cups water
1 (16 oz.) can tomatoes
1 onion, diced
3 carrots, sliced
3 ribs celery, sliced
1 can green beans,
   drained
½ cup barley
1 tsp. sweet basil
¼ medium head
   cabbage, sliced (optional)

1 lb. stew meat, cooked
salt and pepper to taste
1 Tbsp. Worcestershire
   sauce
3 potatoes, peeled
   and diced
10 oz. frozen corn
1 tsp. sugar
1 (10½ oz.) can
   beef consomme

Combine all ingredients and cook
until vegetables are tender, adding
cabbage the last 20 minutes.

Serves 8-10.

SPRING CHICKEN SOUP

So-named because it
is a soup that is especially appropriate for
those still-chilly days in early spring... a little lighter
in substance and appearance than the thick, heavy
stews we associate with winter... yet warm and satisfying.

3-4 oz. macaroni
prepared according to directions and set aside...
1 (14 oz.) can chicken broth
2 (10 ¾ oz.) cans cream of chicken soup
1 cup milk
2 cups chopped ham
1 onion, diced
2 carrots, peeled and sliced
2 ribs celery, diced
½ cup butter
1 (16 oz.) can tomatoes
2 cups cooked chicken, cut into bite-sized pieces
salt and pepper to taste
1 pint Half 'n' Half

In a medium sized bowl, combine macaroni and broth, soup, and milk. Set aside. In a large soup pot, sauté ham, onion, carrots, and celery in the butter. Add broth mixture and simmer over medium-low heat for about 10 minutes. Stir in the tomatoes, chicken and seasoning. Add Half 'n' Half and gently heat through. Serves 8-10. Great with Farmhouse Cheddar Muffins.

60

Potato Soup

1 yellow onion, peeled and diced
½ cup butter or margarine
8 potatoes, peeled and diced
enough water to cover potatoes in the pot
3 Tbsp. chicken bouillon
½ cup flour
4 cups Half 'n' Half or milk
1 Tbsp. dried parsley flakes or
3 Tbsp. fresh parsley, chopped
10 oz. frozen peas
Add, if desired, 1 cup of any or all
of the following vegetables:

sautéed mushrooms	green beans
shredded carrots	3 or 4 strips of bacon,
shredded zucchini	fried until crisp

~salt and pepper to taste

Sauté onion in the butter until clear. Add potatoes and cover with water. Add bouillon and cook over medium-high heat until potatoes are tender. Reduce heat. Combine flour and half of the milk or Half 'n' Half in a jar and shake well to mix. Add to the potatoes and stir for 3-4 minutes, or until thickened. Gradually add remaining milk, stirring constantly to avoid scorching. Add remaining vegetables and seasonings. Gently heat through. Garnish with crumbled, crisp bacon, if desired... Serves 6 - 8.

CORN CHOWDER

½ cup butter or margarine
2 potatoes, peeled and diced
2 ribs celery, minced
2 Tbsp. chopped green or sweet red pepper
1 medium onion, peeled and chopped
2 Tbsp. flour
1 tsp. salt
1 cup water
2 Tbsp. instant chicken bouillon
20 oz. frozen corn
3-4 cups Half 'n' Half or milk

Sauté first five ingredients about 10 minutes, or until almost tender. Blend in the flour and salt. Cook one minute. Stir in the water and bouillon, stirring constantly for 3-4 minutes. Then add corn and milk. Gently heat through. Serves 8.

Key West Chowder

½ cup green onions,
    chopped
1 cup butter
2 cups diced celery
2 cups sliced carrots
4 cups water
parsley

4 Tbsp. chicken bouillon
1 cup flour
3-4 cups half 'n' half
    or milk
1 tsp. seafood seasoning
1 lb. seafood of your
    choice, diced

Sauté onions in butter and flour and
stir 2 minutes over medium heat.
Gradually add half 'n' half,
stirring another 2 minutes.
Set aside.

Bring carrots and celery to
a boil in water and bouillon.
Cook until tender. Add cream
mixture, seasoning and
seafood. Heat through.
Garnish with parsley.

Serves 6-8.

EMILY'S QUICK BEAN SOUP

1½ lbs. ground chuck
1 onion, chopped
3 (10 oz.) cans minestrone
2 (10 oz.) cans Rotel tomatoes and chiles
2 (15 oz.) can Ranch Style Beans

Brown meat with onion
and drain off fat. Combine with
the other ingredients and
simmer for 1 hour.

Settler's Beans

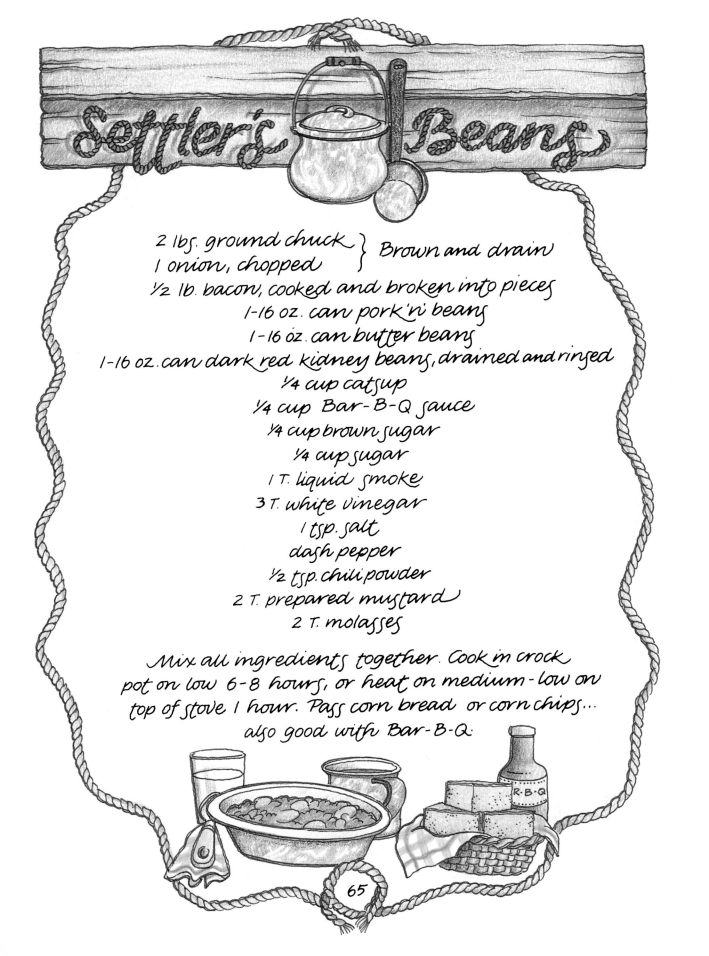

2 lbs. ground chuck   } Brown and drain
1 onion, chopped

½ lb. bacon, cooked and broken into pieces
1-16 oz. can pork 'n' beans
1-16 oz. can butter beans
1-16 oz. can dark red kidney beans, drained and rinsed
¼ cup catsup
¼ cup Bar-B-Q sauce
¼ cup brown sugar
¼ cup sugar
1 T. liquid smoke
3 T. white vinegar
1 tsp. salt
dash pepper
½ tsp. chili powder
2 T. prepared mustard
2 T. molasses

Mix all ingredients together. Cook in crock pot on low 6-8 hours, or heat on medium-low on top of stove 1 hour. Pass corn bread or corn chips... also good with Bar-B-Q.

STEAK SOUP

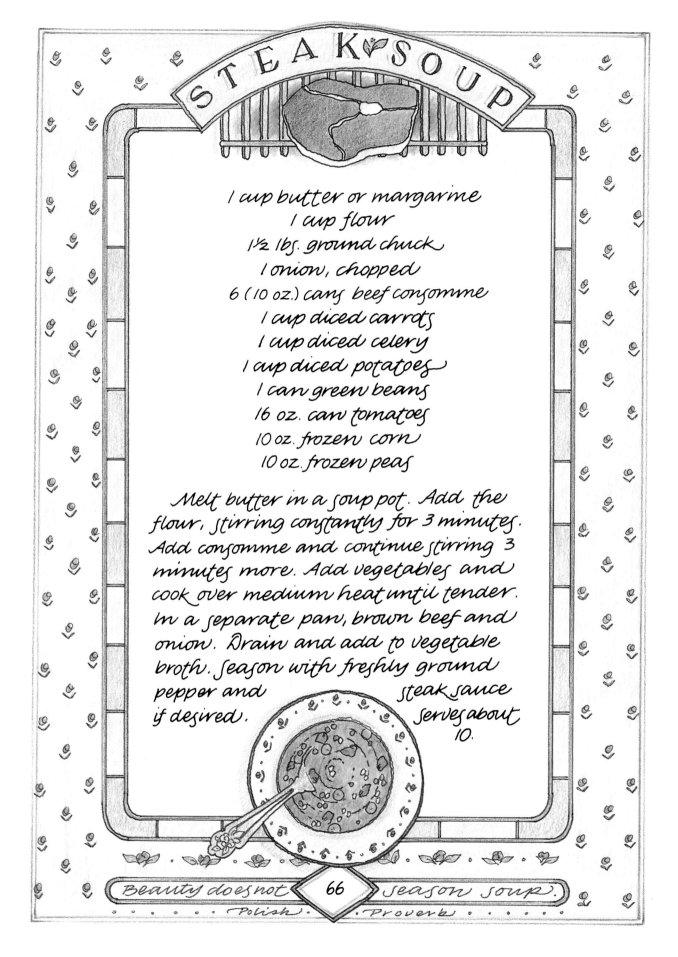

1 cup butter or margarine
1 cup flour
1½ lbs. ground chuck
1 onion, chopped
6 (10 oz.) cans beef consomme
1 cup diced carrots
1 cup diced celery
1 cup diced potatoes
1 can green beans
16 oz. can tomatoes
10 oz. frozen corn
10 oz. frozen peas

Melt butter in a soup pot. Add the flour, stirring constantly for 3 minutes. Add consomme and continue stirring 3 minutes more. Add vegetables and cook over medium heat until tender. In a separate pan, brown beef and onion. Drain and add to vegetable broth. Season with freshly ground pepper and steak sauce if desired. Serves about 10.

Beauty does not season soup.
Polish Proverb

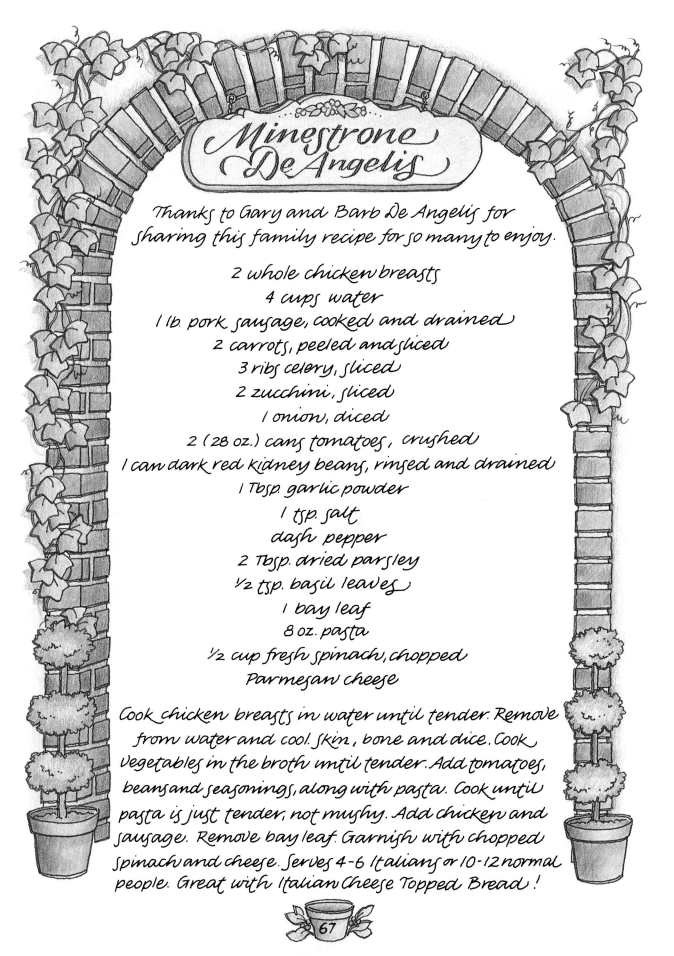

Minestrone De Angelis

Thanks to Gary and Barb De Angelis for
sharing this family recipe for so many to enjoy.

2 whole chicken breasts
4 cups water
1 lb. pork sausage, cooked and drained
2 carrots, peeled and sliced
3 ribs celery, sliced
2 zucchini, sliced
1 onion, diced
2 (28 oz.) cans tomatoes, crushed
1 can dark red kidney beans, rinsed and drained
1 Tbsp. garlic powder
1 tsp. salt
dash pepper
2 Tbsp. dried parsley
½ tsp. basil leaves
1 bay leaf
8 oz. pasta
½ cup fresh spinach, chopped
Parmesan cheese

Cook chicken breasts in water until tender. Remove
from water and cool. Skin, bone and dice. Cook
vegetables in the broth until tender. Add tomatoes,
beans and seasonings, along with pasta. Cook until
pasta is just tender, not mushy. Add chicken and
sausage. Remove bay leaf. Garnish with chopped
spinach and cheese. Serves 4-6 Italians or 10-12 normal
people. Great with Italian Cheese Topped Bread !

Chicken Vegetable
S·O·U·P

1 (6.25 oz.) Uncle Ben's
Instant Long Grain and Wild Rice
3 lbs. chicken, cut up
6 Tbsp. instant chicken bouillon
1 yellow onion, diced
8 oz. fresh mushrooms, sliced
½ cup butter
2 cups diced carrots
2 cups diced celery

Cook chicken in about 8 cups of water over
medium-high heat until tender. Remove from
broth to cool. Skim fat and residue off of the broth.
Add bouillon, carrots and celery to broth and cook
until tender. Add rice and seasoning packet that
comes with the rice. Continue to cook over medium
heat. Sauté mushrooms and onion in the butter. Add
to the broth. Skin and bone chicken and cut into small
pieces. Add   to the broth
and serve.   Serves 6-8.

Chicken Vegetable Soup

Chicken Soup Au Gratin

This recipe comes from Jannie Drover. Jannie and I always meant to enroll in a cooking class together, but somehow it never worked out. I can't make this soup without also remembering Jannie's wonderful in-laws, Jack and Thelma. Their support during my early years in the restaurant business was matchless.

2 chicken breasts, whole
½ tsp. salt
2 cups water
½ cup onion, chopped
½ cup chopped carrots
½ cup diced celery
1 (10 oz.) can cream of chicken soup
½ cup milk or Half 'n' Half
dash of freshly ground pepper
1 cup cheddar cheese, grated

Simmer chicken in the salted water until tender. Remove the skin and bone, and dice. Boil vegetables in the broth until tender. Gradually stir in the soup, milk, and pepper. Add cheese and chicken. Heat through, stirring until cheese melts.

Serves 4

FRENCH MARKET SOUP

20 oz. bean mix
(with seasoning packet if available)
2 Tbsp. salt
28 oz. can tomatoes, crushed
1 large yellow onion, diced
4 ribs celery, diced
2 carrots, peeled and diced
1 clove garlic, crushed
1 lb. smoked sausage, sliced
2 whole chicken breasts, skinned, boned and diced
½ lb. country ham
1 tsp. seasoned salt
1 tsp. freshly ground pepper

Wash beans and drain. Cover with water and salt. Soak overnight. Drain. Add 2-3 quarts water and seasoning packet that came with beans (this package is optional). Simmer for 3 hours. Meanwhile, sauté chicken, ham, and sausage pieces with onion, celery, carrots and garlic. You may want to spray the pan first with a vegetable oil coating. Add seasoned salt and pepper. Add to beans along with crushed tomatoes and simmer an additional 1½ hours uncovered. Should be thick. Freezes well.

Serves 8-10.

Stuffed Spud Soup

2 lbs. frozen hash browns, thawed
½ cup butter
½ cup chopped green onion
1 (10 oz.) can cream of chicken soup
salt and pepper to taste
3-4 cups Half 'n' Half or milk
1 cup shredded cheddar cheese
parsley flakes or chopped chives for garnish

Sauté onion in butter. Add soup, Half 'n' Half, and thawed potatoes. Stir in cheese and heat gently. Garnish and serve.

Serves 8-10.

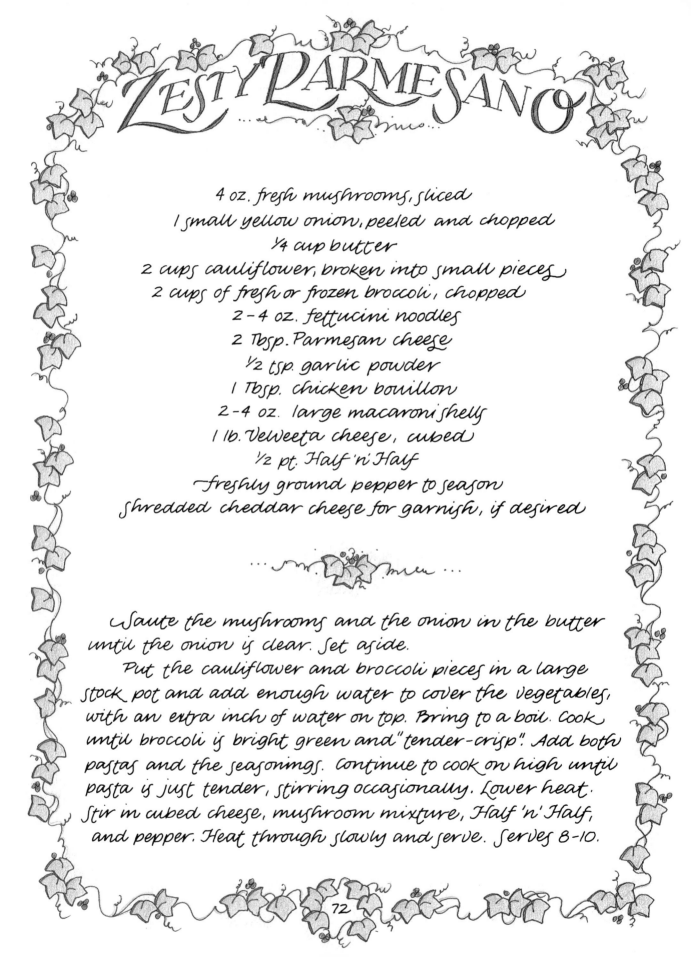

Zesty Parmesano

4 oz. fresh mushrooms, sliced
1 small yellow onion, peeled and chopped
¼ cup butter
2 cups cauliflower, broken into small pieces
2 cups of fresh or frozen broccoli, chopped
2-4 oz. fettucini noodles
2 Tbsp. Parmesan cheese
½ tsp. garlic powder
1 Tbsp. chicken bouillon
2-4 oz. large macaroni shells
1 lb. Velveeta cheese, cubed
½ pt. Half 'n' Half
freshly ground pepper to season
shredded cheddar cheese for garnish, if desired

Saute the mushrooms and the onion in the butter until the onion is clear. Set aside.

Put the cauliflower and broccoli pieces in a large stock pot and add enough water to cover the vegetables, with an extra inch of water on top. Bring to a boil. Cook until broccoli is bright green and "tender-crisp". Add both pastas and the seasonings. Continue to cook on high until pasta is just tender, stirring occasionally. Lower heat. Stir in cubed cheese, mushroom mixture, Half 'n' Half, and pepper. Heat through slowly and serve. Serves 8-10.

WHITE CHILE

1 lb. white beans,
soaked overnight and drained
4 cups chicken broth
1 clove garlic minced
1 onion, diced
1 small can chopped green chiles
scant teaspoon ground cumin
scant teaspoon dried oregano
dash of ground cloves
dash of cayenne pepper
4 cups cooked chicken, diced
3 cups grated Monterey Jack cheese

Combine beans, chicken broth, garlic
and onions in a large soup pot and bring to a
boil. Reduce heat and simmer for 2-3 hours.
Add remaining ingredients, with the
exception of the cheese, and simmer
an additional hour. Garnish
with cheese.
Serves 8-10.

Friendship

"Hold a true friend
with both your hands."

~ Nigerian Proverb

"Friendship is unnecessary,
like philosophy, like art...
It has no survival value;
rather it is one of those things
that gives value to survival.

~ C.S. Lewis

"A man must get friends as he would get
food and drink for nourishment
and sustenance."

~ Randolf Silliman Bourne

"A friend is a present
which you give yourself"

~ Robert Louis Stevenson

Main Dishes

One cannot think well,
love well, sleep well,
if one has not dined well.

~Virginia Wolf

Osage Hills
CHICKEN POT PIE

1 whole chicken (cooked and deboned)
1 can cream of chicken soup
1 can mixed vegetables, drained
1 cup chicken broth
1 recipe for double crust pie crust or prepared pie crust

Dice the cooked chicken into bite size pieces. Mix with the soup, vegetables, and chicken broth. Heat and stir until smooth. This may be done in the microwave or on top of the range. Pour into a 9" unbaked pie shell. Top with another 9" unbaked pie shell. Bake at 350° for about 35-45 minutes or until crust is light golden brown.

Serves 4-6.

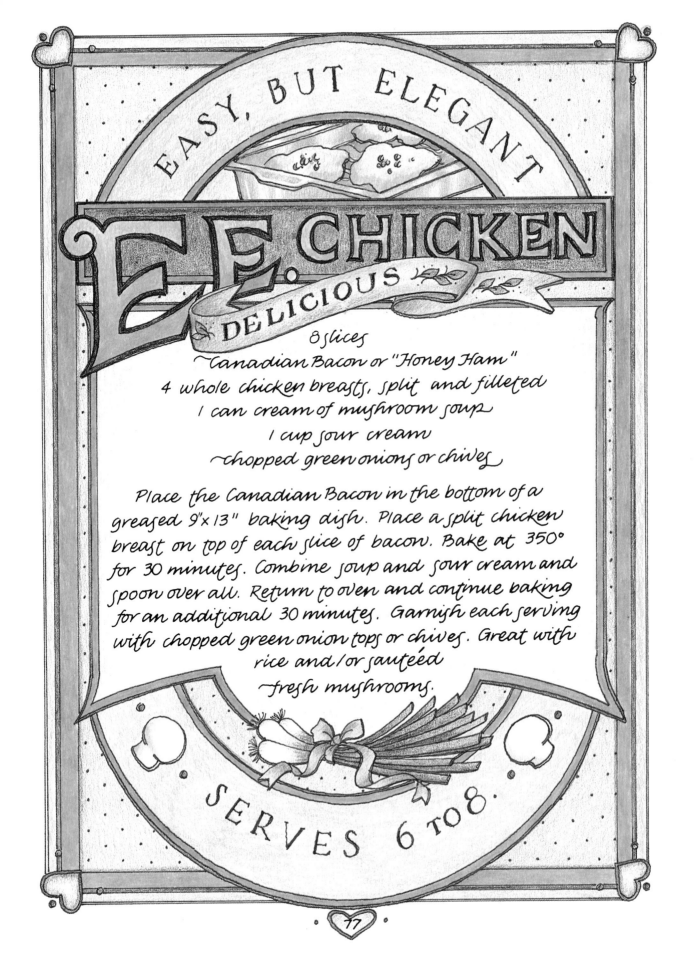

EASY, BUT ELEGANT

E.E. CHICKEN

DELICIOUS

8 slices
Canadian Bacon or "Honey Ham"
4 whole chicken breasts, split and filleted
1 can cream of mushroom soup
1 cup sour cream
chopped green onions or chives

Place the Canadian Bacon in the bottom of a greased 9"x 13" baking dish. Place a split chicken breast on top of each slice of bacon. Bake at 350° for 30 minutes. Combine soup and sour cream and spoon over all. Return to oven and continue baking for an additional 30 minutes. Garnish each serving with chopped green onion tops or chives. Great with rice and/or sautéed fresh mushrooms.

SERVES 6 TO 8

CASHEW CHICKEN

1 cup milk
3 eggs, well beaten
seasoned salt
6 chicken breast halves, cut into bite size pieces
3 Tbsp. cornstarch
2 cups chicken broth
3 Tbsp. Oyster Sauce
(found in the oriental food section of your grocery store)
1 tsp. sugar
ground pepper to taste
2 cups flour
vegetable oil for frying
2 cups cashew nuts
½ cup chopped green onions
soy sauce
fried rice to serve 6

Marinate chicken pieces in milk, eggs, and seasoned
salt for 30 minutes. In a small saucepan, dissolve cornstarch in about ½ cup of the chicken broth. Stir over medium
heat, adding the remaining broth gradually. Blend in oyster
sauce, sugar and pepper. Continue to stir until sauce bubbles
and thickens. Keep on warm setting.
Drain marinade off of chicken. Roll each piece in
flour and then fry in hot oil until golden,
being careful not to crowd. Drain
on paper towels. Serve with fried rice.
Garnish with cashews, onion and
sauce. Pass the soy sauce.
Serves 6.

Chicken Ala King

1 medium fryer chicken, cut up

1 qt. water

1 Tbsp. parsley flakes

2 carrots, peeled and sliced

salt and pepper to taste

½ tsp. basil

Simmer above ingredients for an hour or until meat is tender. Remove from heat. Take the chicken out of stock and remove the skin and bones. Save 2 cups of the broth, and continue with the rest of the recipe.

½ cup butter

1 cup diced celery

4 oz. sliced mushrooms

½ cup flour

2 cups broth

chicken and carrots from above stock

1 (10 oz.) bag frozen peas

1 cup milk

1 pkg. frozen puff pastry shells, prepared according to directions

Melt the butter in a large skillet. Add celery and mushrooms and sauté until tender. Blend in flour and simmer 1 minute. Slowly add chicken broth. Cook about 3-5 minutes, stirring constantly until thick. Add chicken and vegetables and milk. Simmer about 10 minutes, adding peas the last 5 minutes. Spoon chicken mixture into hot pastry shells just before serving.

Serves 6-8

CHICKEN ENCHILADAS

2 Tbsp. butter

1 yellow onion, peeled & diced

1 (16 oz.) can tomatoes, crushed

8 oz. tomato sauce

1 tsp. ground cumin

½ tsp. oregano

8 flour tortillas

1 cup grated Cheddar cheese

1 tsp. minced garlic

2 cups cooked, diced chicken

4 oz. chopped green chiles

1 tsp. sugar

½ tsp. salt

½ tsp. basil

3 cups grated
    Monterey Jack cheese

3/4 cup sour cream

Sauté onion and garlic in butter. Add tomato, chiles, tomato sauce, sugar and spices. Bring to a boil and simmer 20 minutes. Spoon some of the sauce over the tortillas, one at a time to soften a little. Top with a few pieces of chicken breast, and both kinds of cheese, reserving 1 cup of cheese for topping. Roll up and place seam side down in a greased baking dish. Blend sour cream with remaining sauce; pour over top. Sprinkle with remaining cheese. Bake at 350° for 40 minutes.

Serves 4.

80

Chicken Fajita Quesadilla

1 pkg. soft flour tortillas
3 Tbsp. vegetable oil for frying
1 cup shredded cheddar cheese
1 cup shredded Monterey Jack cheese
½ cup chopped green onions
2 cups cooked and diced chicken
1 cup chopped tomatoes
1 small can chopped green chiles, drained
your favorite salsa
8 oz. sour cream

Heat oil in large skillet. Place tortilla in hot oil in skillet, and top with a few tablespoons of each: both cheeses, onions, chicken, tomatoes and green chiles. Then top with another tortilla. Fry until bottom tortilla is slightly browned. Turn and brown other tortilla. Remove from skillet and keep warm until serving. Repeat with remaining tortillas. Cut into wedges and serve with salsa and sour cream on the side. May also be served as an appetizer.

Serves 4-6.

Vegetable Stroganoff

⅓ cup sour cream
1½ cups plain yogurt
½ cup V-8 or tomato juice
1 cup diced onion
8 oz. fresh mushrooms, sliced
¼ tsp. dill weed
paprika, salt and pepper to taste
6 cups fresh vegetables, steamed (broccoli,
cauliflower, carrots, celery, peppers, zucchini, etc. ~
~ a combination of any or all of these is best.)

4 cups hot, cooked noodles

Sauté onion and mushrooms in butter until onions
are soft. Combine with seasonings, sour cream, yogurt
and juice and heat gently. To serve, layer
hot noodles, then hot vegetables,
~and then sauce.

~Makes about 4 servings.

Pasta Con Broccoli

1 (8 oz.) box Cavatelli
4 oz. fresh mushrooms, sliced
1 tsp. crushed garlic
½ cup butter
1 pint heavy cream
2 cups Grated Parmesan Cheese
2 bunches broccoli,
cut into pieces and cook until tender crisp
salt and pepper to taste

Sauté the mushrooms and the garlic in
2 Tablespoons of the butter. Set aside. Melt the
remaining 6 Tablespoons of the butter. Slowly
add the cream and the cheese. Stir until
the cheese is melted. Add broccoli and
mushrooms. Prepare the Cavatelli
according to the package directions.
After draining, add sauce
and serve.

6~8 Servings

Classic

ROAST BEEF DINNER

1 (2-3 lb.) boneless roast
1 (10 oz.) can French onion soup
4-5 potatoes, peeled and cut into wedges
4-5 carrots, peeled and cut into 1" pieces
seasoned salt and pepper
8 oz. fresh mushrooms, optional

Place roast in a large baking dish. Season. Cover with French onion soup, undiluted. Surround with fresh mushrooms. Bake at 350° for about one hour. Meanwhile cook potatoes and carrots in a little water until just tender. Reserve ½ cup of the water in which the vegetables were cooked. Add this ½ cup liquid and the potatoes and carrots to the roast. Bake an additional 20-30 minutes. When roast has reached the desired "doneness", transfer to a platter and surround with vegetables. Put juice in a gravy boat or a bowl.

Serves 6-8.

"OUR PRAYERS SHOULD BE FOR BLESSINGS IN GENERAL, FOR GOD KNOWS BEST WHAT IS GOOD FOR US."
· SOCRATES ·

BEEF STROGANOFF

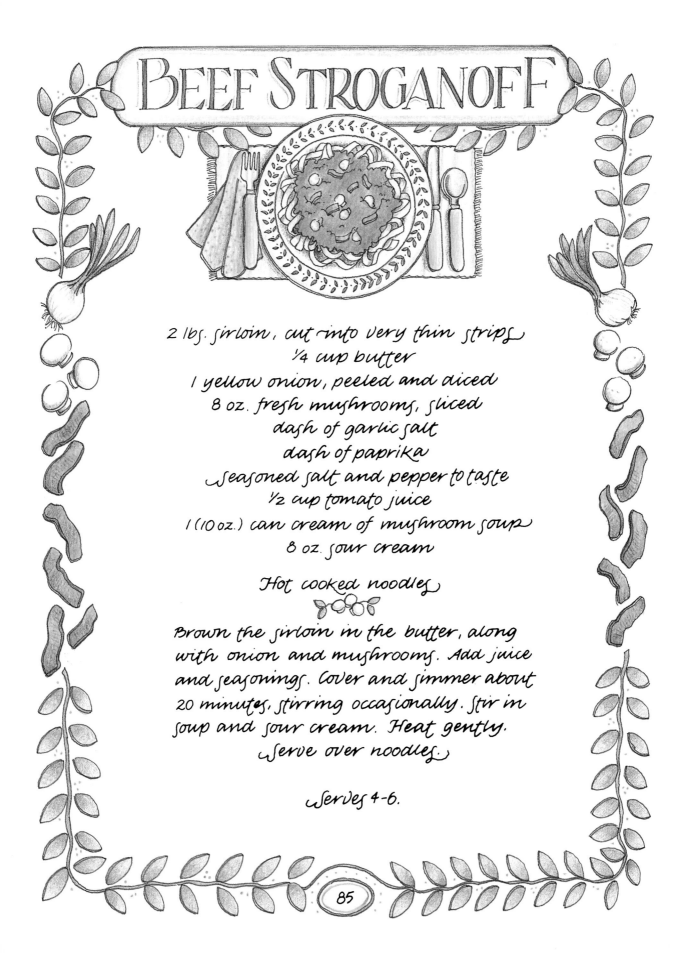

2 lbs. sirloin, cut into very thin strips
¼ cup butter
1 yellow onion, peeled and diced
8 oz. fresh mushrooms, sliced
dash of garlic salt
dash of paprika
seasoned salt and pepper to taste
½ cup tomato juice
1 (10 oz.) can cream of mushroom soup
8 oz. sour cream

Hot cooked noodles

Brown the sirloin in the butter, along
with onion and mushrooms. Add juice
and seasonings. Cover and simmer about
20 minutes, stirring occasionally. Stir in
soup and sour cream. Heat gently.
Serve over noodles.

Serves 4-6.

OVERNIGHT BREAKFAST STRATA

6 slices white or wheat bread
2 1/4 cups shredded Cheddar cheese
1 cup chopped cooked ham
5 eggs
2 Tbsp. green onion, sliced
3/4 tsp. dry mustard
3/4 tsp. Worcestershire sauce
1/4 tsp. garlic powder
dash cayenne
salt and pepper to taste
1 3/4 cup milk

Trim crusts from bread. Butter slices lightly and fit into buttered 7" x 11" dish. Sprinkle with 1 1/2 cups cheese. Top with ham. Mix eggs, onion, mustard, etc. together and pour over layered ingredients. Cover and refrigerate 8 hours or overnight. Bake uncovered at 350° for 30 minutes. Then top with remaining cheese. Bake an additional 10 minutes or until center appears to be set. Let stand 5 minutes before cutting.

6-8 servings

EIGHT LAYER ·QUICHE·

1 deep dish pie shell (frozen or your recipe)
¼ cup chopped green pepper
¼ cup chopped green onion
4 oz. mushrooms, sliced
½ lb. sausage
½ lb. ham, cut into small pieces
4 strips bacon diced
2 chicken breasts, cut into small pieces
1 cup Cheddar cheese, shredded
4 eggs
1 pint Half 'n' Half
2 Tbsp. flour

Sauté the pepper, onion, mushrooms, sausage, ham, bacon, and chicken together in a large skillet. Simmer for about 6-8 minutes. Drain and place in the bottom of the unbaked pie shell. Top with cheese. In a separate bowl, beat the eggs. Add the Half 'n' Half and the flour to the eggs and mix until smooth. Pour into pie shell. Bake at 450° for 10 minutes. Reduce oven temperature to 350° and continue baking 20-25 minutes longer or until set. Serves 6.

S T I R · F R Y

Choose any meat and combination of vegetables from this list (or add any favorites of your own) to create your stir fry dish. All ingredients should be bite size and thinly sliced.

Chicken breast pieces
sliced beef or pork
shrimp
broccoli
cauliflower

onion
celery
zucchini
carrots
green pepper

Coat the bottom of a large frying pan or wok with vegetable oil or peanut oil. Heat oil. Add meat. Season lightly, if desired, with salt. Cook and stir until tender, but not brown. Add vegetables and continue stirring and cooking on medium-high heat until the vegetables are tender-crisp. A bottled stir fry or teriyaki sauce may be added at this time. ~ if you wish. Heat through.

Serve with rice and pass the soy sauce.

Buttery Baked Fish

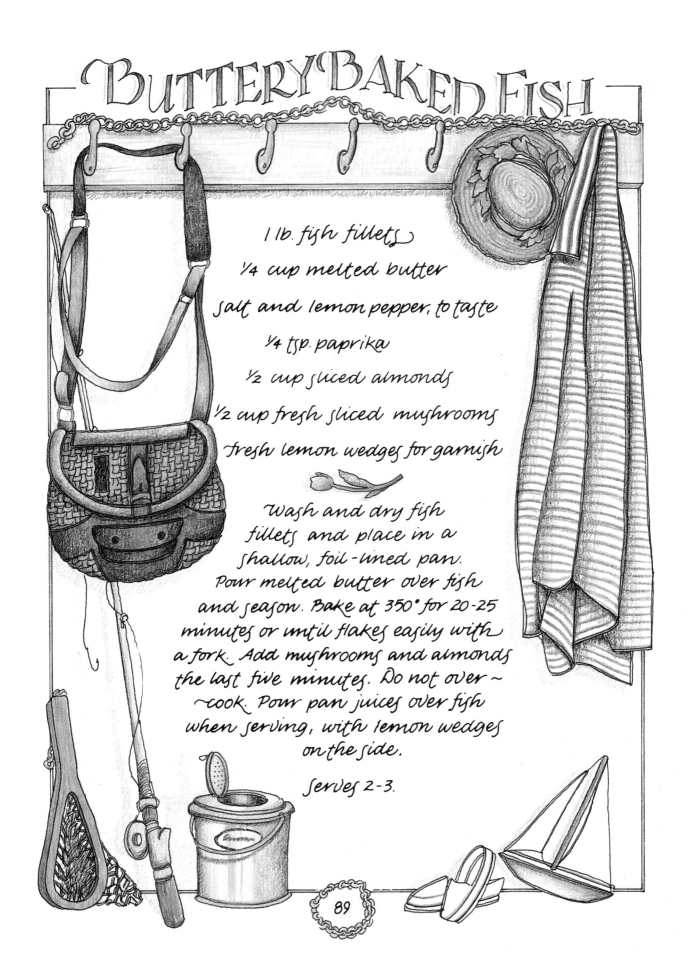

1 lb. fish fillets

¼ cup melted butter

salt and lemon pepper, to taste

¼ tsp. paprika

½ cup sliced almonds

½ cup fresh sliced mushrooms

fresh lemon wedges for garnish

Wash and dry fish fillets and place in a shallow, foil-lined pan. Pour melted butter over fish and season. Bake at 350° for 20-25 minutes or until flakes easily with a fork. Add mushrooms and almonds the last five minutes. Do not over~ ~cook. Pour pan juices over fish when serving, with lemon wedges on the side.

Serves 2-3.

Jan's BAKED LASAGNE

Everyone should be blessed
with a sister like my sister, Jan. There are no
words to adequately express the depths of my love
for her... As you prepare this recipe, think about
the "sisters" (biologically or otherwise) in your life.
As the sauce simmers, pick up the phone, and let
one of them know that you
love her.

1½ lbs. ground chuck
1 small onion, peeled and diced
28 oz. can tomatoes, crushed
12 oz. can tomato paste
1 Tbsp. sugar
1 tsp. salt
½ tsp. oregano
½ tsp. thyme
½ tsp. crushed red pepper
¼ tsp. garlic salt
bay leaf
8 oz. lasagne noodles
2 eggs
15 oz. Ricotta cheese
16 oz. Mozzarella cheese

Brown ground chuck with onion and drain. Combine first four ingredients and spices. Simmer 30 minutes, covered, stirring occasionally. Discard bay leaf. Prepare noodles according to package directions. Arrange a layer of noodles in a greased 9"x 13" baking dish, combine eggs and Ricotta cheese, mixing well. Spoon half of this mixture over noodles. Then spoon half of meat and half of Mozzarella over the Ricotta mixture. Repeat with noodles, cheeses and meat again. Bake at 375° for 45 minutes. Let stand for 10 minutes before cutting. Try this with the Italian Salad (p.48) and the Italian Cheese Topped Bread (p.28). Serves 6-8.

While many of us are busy building, (empires, businesses, etc.), my friend, Janet Baker is busy planting... although she doesn't have an actual garden that I'm aware of, she is always planting seeds and nurturing and cultivating and helping someone grow into their strongest self. We have "broken bread" with the Bakers many times, and thanks to Janet, in addition to the Garden Party Fondue (p.2), we sometimes have...

Janet's GARDEN · PARTY · SANDWICH

1 loaf French Bread,
sliced in half lengthwise

¼ cup zesty Italian dressing	4 oz. Mozzarella cheese, sliced
4 oz. Cheddar cheese, sliced	¼ cup Thousand Island dressing
4 oz. sliced ham	4 oz. sliced roast beef
4 oz. sliced turkey	lettuce
tomato	sliced onion, optional

Spread Italian dressing on the top half of bread. Top with cheeses. Broil until cheese melts. Spread Thousand Island dressing on the bottom half and top with meats and vegetables. Join the top with the bottom, and slice diagonally every 2". Serves 4-6.

"Oh, Adam was a gardener, and God who made him sees
That half a proper gardener's work is done upon his knees."
~ Rudyard Kipling

Love   Peace   Joy   Patience   Kindness   Goodness   Faithfulness   Gentleness   Self-Control

Hot Potato Salad

8 potatoes
1 lb. Velveeta cheese, cut into chunks
1 cup mayonnaise
½ cup chopped onion
salt and pepper to taste
½ cup sliced black olives, optional
½ lb. bacon, cooked and crumbled

Boil the potatoes in water with the skins on until just tender (not mushy!). Peel and cut into chunks. Toss with cheese, mayonnaise and onion. Arrange in a 2 quart baking dish. Season. Top with olives and bacon. Bake at 350° for 1 hour.

Serves 6-8.

H·E·R·B·E·D
POTATO
Wedges

CILANTRO

ENGLISH THYME

BAY LEAF

ROSEMARY

4 potatoes, scrubbed ~
and cut into eighths, lengthwise
½ cup butter
4 oz. Parmesan cheese
4 strips of crisp bacon, crumbled
freshly ground pepper
½ tsp. rosemary
½ tsp. parsley flakes
½ tsp. thyme
seasoned salt to taste

2 Tbsp. chives
1 cup sour cream

SAGE

FLAT-LEAF PARSLEY

TARRAGON

CHIVES

Melt butter in a large, shallow
baking dish. Arrange potatoes in a
single layer over the butter. Sprinkle
with cheese, bacon and seasonings.
Bake at 350° for 30 minutes. Take
out of oven and baste with butter.
Return to oven and bake until
tender (about 20-30 minutes more).
Mix chives into sour cream and
serve on the side.

Serves 6-8.

BASIL

FRENCH THYME

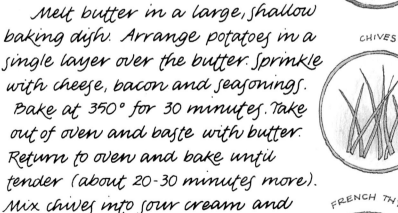

95

ZUCCHINI~ POTATO PANCAKE

1 lb. grated, unpeeled potatoes
½ lb grated, unpeeled zucchini ~ (squeezed dry)
1 egg beaten
2 Tbsp. flour
½ tsp. salt
¼ tsp. nutmeg
freshly ground pepper
1 Tbsp. butter, or more
1 Tbsp. oil, or more

Soak the potatoes in cold water and squeeze dry. Toss the potatoes and zucchini together. Mix the egg, flour, salt, nutmeg and pepper into the potatoes and zucchini. Turn mixture into a large, hot skillet that has been coated with the butter and oil. Fry until golden brown. Flip out onto plate and serve. No need to brown both sides.

Serves about 4.

VEGETABLE MEDLEY
Au Gratin

2 cups cauliflower pieces
2 cups broccoli pieces
4 oz. Velveeta cheese
¼ cup crushed, seasoned salad croutons
1 ripe tomato, diced

* * *

Steam cauliflower and broccoli until tender-crisp. Cut cheese into 1" cubes and arrange over the vegetables in a baking dish. Sprinkle with the crushed croutons and diced tomatoes. Bake in a 350° oven for 15 minutes.

Serves 4-6.

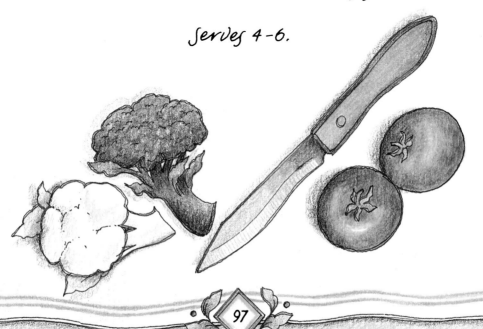

ORIENTAL RICE CASSEROLE

1 onion, peeled and diced
1 green pepper, diced
1 cup celery, diced
¼ cup butter
1 lb. pork sausage, browned and drained
1 cup uncooked rice
3 pkgs. instant chicken noodle soup mix (individual servings)
3 cups boiling water
½ cup blanched almonds

Sauté onions, green pepper, and celery in butter.
Combine with remaining ingredients in a large
casserole dish. Cover and bake 1 hour at 325°.
Remove cover and bake an additional 20-30
minutes.

Serves 4-6.

Rice Medley

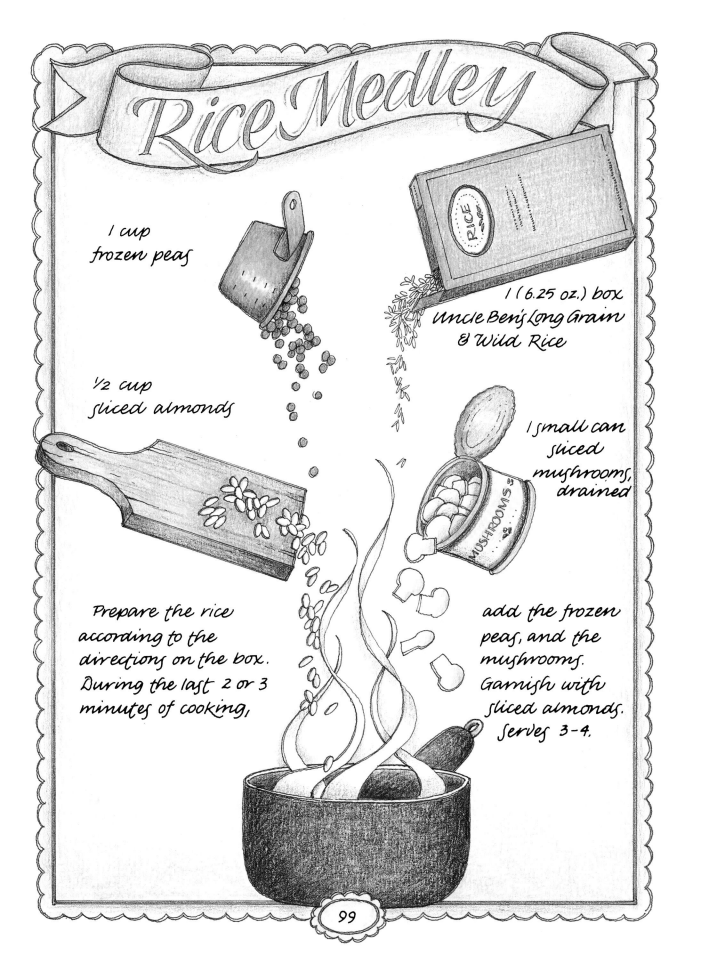

1 cup
frozen peas

1 (6.25 oz.) box
Uncle Ben's Long Grain
& Wild Rice

½ cup
sliced almonds

1 small can
sliced
mushrooms,
drained

Prepare the rice
according to the
directions on the box.
During the last 2 or 3
minutes of cooking,
add the frozen
peas, and the
mushrooms.
Garnish with
sliced almonds.
Serves 3-4.

The ACCESSORY MEAT PIE

16 oz. cream cheese, softened
1½ cups butter
1½ cups margarine
6-7 cups flour
1 lb. ground chuck
1 lb. ground sausage
2 small packages spaghetti mix
1 can black olives, chopped
1 small can mushrooms, chopped
12 oz. cheddar cheese, shredded

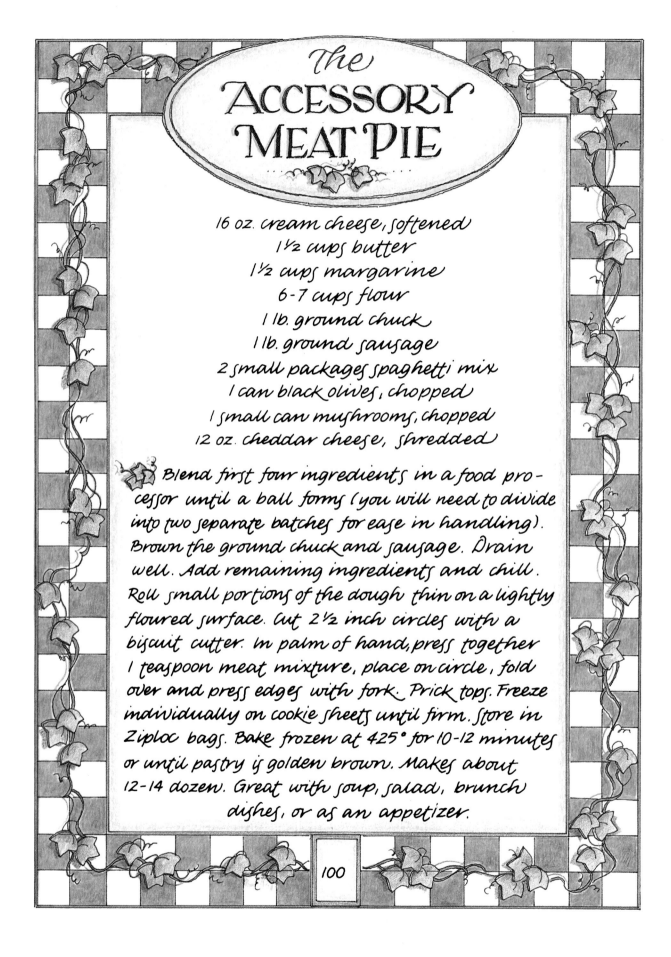 Blend first four ingredients in a food processor until a ball forms (you will need to divide into two separate batches for ease in handling). Brown the ground chuck and sausage. Drain well. Add remaining ingredients and chill. Roll small portions of the dough thin on a lightly floured surface. Cut 2½ inch circles with a biscuit cutter. In palm of hand, press together 1 teaspoon meat mixture, place on circle, fold over and press edges with fork. Prick tops. Freeze individually on cookie sheets until firm. Store in Ziploc bags. Bake frozen at 425° for 10-12 minutes or until pastry is golden brown. Makes about 12-14 dozen. Great with soup, salad, brunch dishes, or as an appetizer.

"...Squash, Anyone?..."

2 lbs. yellow summer squash, sliced
1 medium onion, chopped fine
1 cup shredded carrot
1 cup sour cream
1 can cream of chicken soup
½ cup margarine, melted
1 (8 oz.) pkg. Pepperidge Farm stuffing mix

Parboil squash and drain thoroughly. Combine onion, carrot, sour cream and soup. Fold in squash. Toss melted margarine with stuffing and spread half in bottom of 12" x 7" x 2" baking dish. Spoon vegetable mixture on top. Sprinkle with remaining stuffing. Bake at 350° for 30 minutes.

Serves 8-10.

I had a very special relationship with Marie Hammett. It began one extremely hot day in August when she came to the restaurant to apply for a job as our dishwasher. She was 65 years old then.

As she stood over the sink of steamy water, her white hair clung to her damp forehead. One of the younger, less insightful waitresses whispered to me, "She won't last a week here". Several million dirty dishes and five years later (long after the younger waitress had gone), Marie was "promoted" to the position of NANNY when our son, Blake, was born.

On any given day, she could be seen pushing Blake in his stroller around the little shopping village where our bakery and restaurant were located, spending her paycheck on "necessities" for him (infant sunglasses, countless articles of clothing, remote control cars that he would "grow into someday"). I remember saying to her more than once, "Marie, you're too good to be true. I've decided you must be an angel in disguise".

Another hot day in August, one month before the birth of our daughter, Marie left this world to meet her Maker. If indeed, God does allow his angels to come back to earth, I believe that Marie drops in from time to time to kiss my children while they lay sleeping. Or, perhaps she's hovering over your shoulder.
Thank You, sweet Marie.

Marie Hammett
March 7, 1918 – August 21, 1990

MARIE'S APPLE BUTTER

12 cups apples, peeled and sliced
6 cups sugar
3 cups water
2 Tbsp. cinnamon

Combine all ingredients in a large roasting pan and cover. Bake at 300° for 1 hour. Stir well. Turn oven up to 350° and continue baking (and stirring every half hour) until "butter" is dark brown. Put in sterilized jars and seal.

MAIN ST.

"Be careful lest ye
be entertaining angels
unaware..."

Hebrews 13:2

Baked Potato Topping

½ cup butter, softened
½ cup sour cream
1 cup Cheddar cheese, shredded
2 Tbsp. green onions, chopped
3 slices bacon, cooked until crisp,
and crumbled

Mix butter and sour cream. Fold in cheese, onion, and bacon. Serve at room temperature on baked potatoes.
4-6 servings.

Cakes & Pies

"There is a charm about the forbidden that makes it unspeakably desirable."

—Mark Twain

Gooey Butter Cake

1 box yellow cake mix
1 egg
1 stick butter, melted
8 ounces cream cheese, softened
2 eggs, beaten
2 cups powdered sugar and some for garnish

Blend cake mix, 1 egg, and butter until smooth. Press into a 9"x 13" greased baking pan. Blend cream cheese, 2 eggs, and powdered sugar until creamy and smooth. Spread cream cheese mixture over first mixture in the pan. Bake at 325° for 40-45 minutes or until edges are brown. The middle will "sink" a little. This is normal. Sprinkle with powdered sugar. Serves 10-12.

Welcome Guests

A Tea Party

Ann

Sour Cream
COFFEE CAKE

1 cup butter, softened
2 cups sugar
2 eggs
1 tsp. vanilla
1 tsp. salt
1 tsp. baking powder
2 cups cake flour
1 cup sour cream

Cream butter, sugar and eggs. Fold in sour cream and vanilla. Fold in dry ingredients. Spoon half of batter into greased bundt or tube pan. Cover with filling:

½ cup chopped pecans
1 tsp. cinnamon   ½ cup brown sugar

Spoon remaining batter over cinnamon-nut filling. Bake 1 hour in 350° oven. Remove from pan after 10-15 minutes and sprinkle with powdered sugar.
Serves 10-12.

Festive Fruit Shortcake

2½ cups flour
1 tsp. baking powder
½ tsp. salt
} Mix and set aside.

1½ cups butter
1 lb. powdered sugar
} Cream together.

6 eggs
} Add one at a time, beating well after each addition.
(total beating time: 10 minutes)

and 2 tsp. vanilla

Add dry ingredients. Pour into greased tube or bundt pan. Bake at 350° 50-55 minutes. Let cool 10-15 minutes before removing from pan.

2 cups sliced peaches
2 cups sliced strawberries
2 cups fresh or canned pineapple chunks
1 bunch seedless grapes, halved
2-3 bananas, sliced

Toss all fruit together and store in refrigerator. This will be used to top slices of pound cake. Whipped cream and sliced almonds may be used for garnish.

Banana Nut CAKE

½ cup butter, softened
1½ cups sugar
2 eggs, beaten
3 ripe bananas, mashed
½ cup chopped pecans
¼ cup buttermilk
2 cups flour
½ tsp. salt
1 tsp. baking soda

Cream butter and sugar until light.
Add eggs, mashed bananas pecans and buttermilk.
Mix dry ingredients and add to banana mixture. Pour into a greased bundt pan, or a 9" x 13" baking pan. Bake at 325° for 1 hour.
When cool, frost with Banana Nut Icing:

Banana Nut ICING

Blend below ingredients well and spread on cooled cake.

¼ cup butter, softened
1 banana, mashed
1 lb. powdered sugar
½ cup pecans, chopped
½ tsp. vanilla

Country Life Carrot Cake

2 cups, plus 1 Tbsp. flour
2 cups sugar
2 tsp. baking soda
2 tsp. cinnamon
1 tsp. salt
1½ cups vegetable oil
4 eggs, beaten
3 cups grated, peeled carrots

Mix dry ingredients in mixer bowl. Add remaining ingredients and beat on medium speed for about 2 minutes. Spread in a greased 9" x 13" baking pan or two greased 8" round pans. Bake at 350° for 30-35 minutes, or until pick inserted in center comes out clean. Frost, when cool, with cream cheese frosting (see next page). Garnish with pecan halves or pieces, if desired.

Serves 10-12

Cream Cheese Frosting

8 oz. cream cheese, softened
½ cup butter, softened
1½ lbs. powdered sugar
1 tsp. vanilla

Blend cream cheese and butter well. Gradually add powdered sugar and beat until smooth. Add vanilla and blend well.

Italian CREAM CAKE

2 cups sugar	½ cup butter
½ cup margarine	5 eggs, separated
1 tsp. baking soda	1 cup buttermilk
2 cups flour	½ tsp. salt
1 Tbsp. vanilla	1 cup coconut

1 cup chopped pecans

Stir soda into buttermilk. Let sit 10 minutes. Cream sugar, butter and margarine until smooth. Add egg yolks, one at a time, beating well after each. Stir together flour and salt. Add alternately with buttermilk to butter mixture. Add vanilla, coconut and pecans. Beat egg whites until stiff. Fold into batter. Pour into three greased and floured 9" cake pans. Bake at 325° for 30-35 minutes, or until cake springs back when touched in the center.
Frost with Cream Cheese Frosting (see previous page).

TEXAS Sheet Cake

1 cup butter, melted

¼ cup cocoa

1 cup water

2 cups flour

1½ cups brown sugar

1 tsp. baking soda

1 tsp. cinnamon

½ tsp. salt

1 (14 oz.) can sweetened condensed milk

2 eggs

1 tsp. vanilla

Mix melted butter, cocoa and water in a saucepan or microwave-proof container. Bring to a boil, and then set aside. Combine flour, brown sugar, baking soda, salt, and cinnamon. Add cocoa mixture and beat well. Stir in ⅓ cup sweetened condensed milk, eggs and vanilla. Pour into a greased 15"x 10" baking pan. Bake at 350° for 15 minutes or until cake springs back when lightly touched. When cool, frost with this Chocolate Icing:

Chocolate Icing

Mix butter, cocoa, milk and powdered sugar until smooth and creamy. Spread on cake and garnish with pecans.

¼ cup butter melted

¼ cup cocoa

remaining sweetened condensed milk from above can

1 cup powdered sugar

1 cup pecans, chopped

BANANA SPLIT CAKE

2 cups graham cracker crumbs
½ cup butter, melted

> Mix well and press into a 9" x 13" pan. Set aside.

1 box instant vanilla pudding

> Prepare pudding according to package directions and spread over crust

...THEN LAYER...

5 bananas, sliced
1 small can crushed pineapple, drained
1 can strawberry pie filling
1 large carton Cool Whip
1 cup chopped pecans
maraschino cherries, if desired

Refrigerate several hours. Serve with ice cream.
Serves 10-12.

COLONIAL PUMPKIN BARS

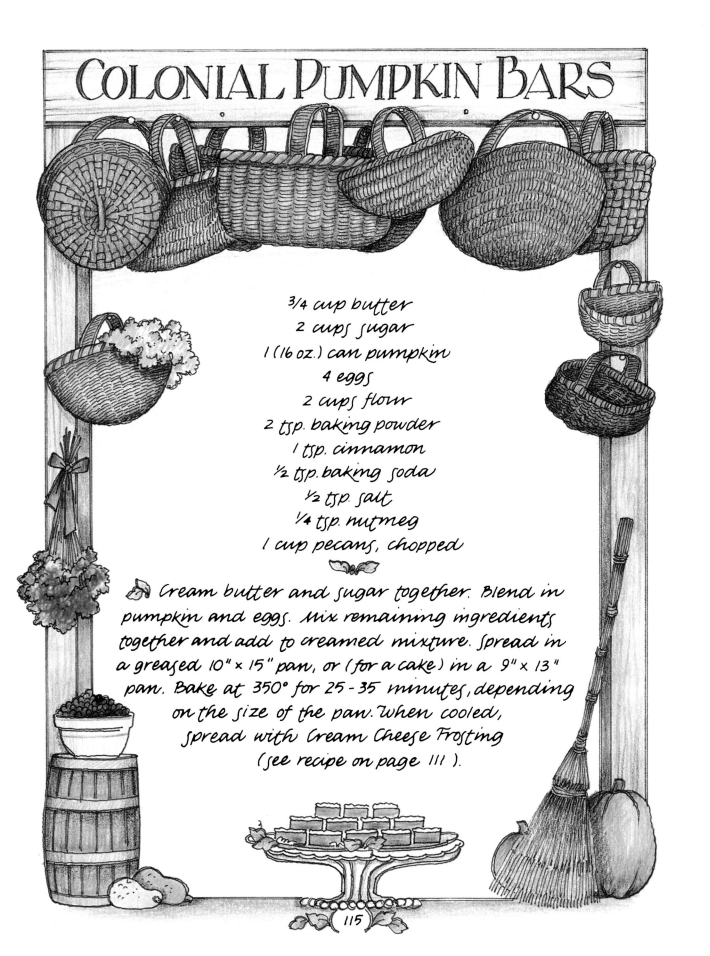

3/4 cup butter
2 cups sugar
1 (16 oz.) can pumpkin
4 eggs
2 cups flour
2 tsp. baking powder
1 tsp. cinnamon
½ tsp. baking soda
½ tsp. salt
¼ tsp. nutmeg
1 cup pecans, chopped

Cream butter and sugar together. Blend in pumpkin and eggs. Mix remaining ingredients together and add to creamed mixture. Spread in a greased 10" x 15" pan, or (for a cake) in a 9" x 13" pan. Bake at 350° for 25 - 35 minutes, depending on the size of the pan. When cooled, spread with Cream Cheese Frosting (see recipe on page 111).

115

English Walnut
CHEESECAKE

Although I'm not usually a "walnut fan", this
is probably my favorite cheesecake. Put aside your
prejudices about walnuts and try it — you may
be a convert as well.

Crust:

1 cup graham cracker
   crumbs
¼ cup butter, melted
2 Tbsp. sugar

Mix well and press
into the bottom of
a 10" or 12"
springform pan.

Filling:

7 (8oz.) pkgs. cream cheese, softened
1¼ cups brown sugar
4 eggs, lightly beaten
1½ tsp. vanilla
6 Tbsp. flour, tossed with 1½ cups finely chopped walnuts
whipped cream and walnut halves for garnish

Blend cream cheese until smooth. Add brown
sugar and mix thoroughly. Add eggs and then vanilla. Fold in walnuts and flour. Pour batter evenly
over crust. Bake until lightly golden, about 60-65
minutes in a 350° oven. Let cool on rack 1 hour. Remove
springform side of pan and chill for at least 2 hours.
Garnish and serve. 10-12 servings.

Chocolate Chip CHEESECAKE

3 (8 oz.) pkgs. cream cheese, softened
1 can sweetened condensed milk
3 eggs
2 tsp. vanilla
1½ cups mini chocolate chips
2 tsp. flour
20 chocolate sandwich cookies
(I use Oreos or Hydrox)

Blend cream cheese, sweetened condensed milk, eggs and vanilla until smooth. Toss chocolate chips with flour and fold into cheese mixture. Set aside while preparing crust. To make crust, crush cookies in a food processor or blender until fine. Press into the bottom of a 10" springform pan. Pour cheesecake batter over the crust. Bake in 300° oven for 1 hour or until set. Cool completely. Chill for at least 1 hour before serving. Garnish with whipped cream and chocolate shavings.

Serves 8-10.

117

APPLE STRUDEL
· Cheese Pie ·

Wayne Gmachl (no, that is not a typo – he really does spell his name like that) ate lunch at our restaurant many times when he found himself in the lake area on business. After each meal, I would say, "Wayne, how was your meal?" He would always respond, "Great. But my wife makes the most spectacular dessert ... you have to try it someday." And one day, he just walked in the back door with this "most spectacular dessert" in one hand and the recipe in the other. Thanks, Leslie and Wayne!

16 oz. cream cheese, softened
½ cup sugar
2 eggs
1 tsp. vanilla
4-5 tart apples, peeled and sliced
(toss sliced apples in 1 tsp. cinnamon and ¼ cup sugar)
1 unbaked pie shell

Toppings

5 Tbsp. sugar   2 Tbsp. butter
2 Tbsp. flour   ½ tsp. cinnamon
Blend these ingredients until coarse.

Blend cream cheese, sugar, eggs and vanilla until smooth. Pour into an unbaked pie shell. Top with apple slices in a "spiral" fashion, then sprinkle with topping. Bake at 450° for 10 minutes. Then reduce oven temperature to 350° and continue baking an additional 30 minutes or until set. Cool. Chill for at least 1 hour before serving.
Serves 6-8.

German Chocolate CHEESECAKE

Crust:

1 cup graham cracker crumbs
2 Tbsp. sugar
3 Tbsp. butter, melted

Mix and press into the bottom of a 10" springform pan.

Cheese Filling:

24 oz. cream cheese, softened
3/4 cup sugar
1/4 cup cocoa
2 tsp. vanilla
3 eggs, beaten

Blend cream cheese, sugar, cocoa, and vanilla. Add eggs, slowly. Pour over crust. Bake at 350° for 35 minutes. When completely cooled, spread on topping.

Topping:

2 Tbsp. butter
1/4 cup evaporated milk
2 Tbsp. brown sugar
1 egg yolk, beaten
1/2 tsp. vanilla
1/2 cup chopped pecans
1/2 cup coconut

Melt butter over low heat. Blend in milk, sugar, egg yolk, and vanilla. Cook, stirring constantly, until thickened. Stir in pecans and coconut and spread on cooled cheesecake.

This becomes an extra nice dessert when you shave some chocolate on top, dust with a little powdered sugar and "dot" with a cherry.

Cheesecake Miniatures

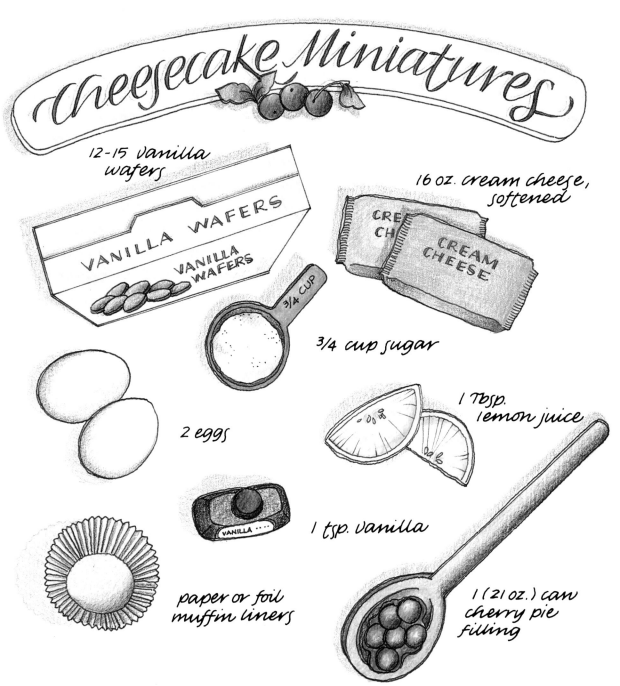

12-15 Vanilla wafers

16 oz. cream cheese, softened

3/4 cup sugar

2 eggs

1 Tbsp. lemon juice

1 tsp. vanilla

paper or foil muffin liners

1 (21 oz.) can cherry pie filling

Place a wafer in the bottom of each liner in a muffin tin. Blend cream cheese and sugar together. Add eggs, lemon juice and vanilla and beat until smooth. Fill liners 2/3 full. Bake at 350° for about 15-18 minutes or until set. Cool. Remove from pan. Top with fruit filling. Store in refrigerator until serving time.

Mom's Easy Apple Crisp

Thanks to Sunny Krehbiel's mom for this fast and fun recipe...

6 apples, peeled and sliced
½ cup sugar
2 tsp. lemon juice
½ tsp. cinnamon
¼ cup water

Mix together and put into an 8" x 8" baking pan.

½ cup packed brown sugar
¾ cup flour
¼ tsp. salt
6 Tbsp. butter, melted

Mix dry ingredients and add butter, mixing until coarse. Crumble over apples and bake at 375° for 40 minutes.

Sunny recommends serving this warm with vanilla ice cream.

Rick's

· A P P L E · P I E ·

I'm not absolutely sure, but I think I may have the best brother-in-law in the whole world. Sometimes, when I'm visiting Jan and Rick in St. Louis he spoils me with this wonderful apple pie.

D O U B L E · P I E · C R U S T

2½ cups all-purpose flour

1 tsp. salt

1 cup vegetable shortening

¼ cup ice water

1 egg, beaten

1 Tbsp. white vinegar

Combine flour and salt in a large bowl. Mix well. With a pastry blender, cut in the shortening until evenly distributed. In a small bowl, combine ice water, egg and vinegar. Sprinkle water mixture over combined dry ingredients, and mix until dough barely clings together. Divide dough for bottom and top crusts. Roll out dough to desired thickness between two sheets of lightly floured wax paper. Put bottom crust in pie pan without stretching dough. Roll out top crust in similar fashion, keeping wax paper on dough until pie is filled to keep from drying out ~ Next page....

APPLE · PIE · FILLING

8 or 9 tart cooking apples, pared
3/4 cup sugar, more if desired
6 Tbsp. flour
1 tsp. cinnamon
1 tsp. nutmeg
2 Tbsp. butter

In a small bowl, combine flour, sugar, cinnamon and nutmeg. Sprinkle about 1/4 cup of mixture on the bottom of the pie crust and add the rest to the apples. Stir to coat apples. Fill pie crust heaping full of apple mixture, dot with butter. Place top crust over filling, flute edges. Cut slits on top crust and sprinkle with sugar. Bake about 50 minutes at 400°. Serve with —vanilla ice cream.

CHERRY PIE

One of the best things
about Jo Ellen's recipe, aside from the
wonderful end results, is that it takes
less than 30 minutes preparation time
from start to finish...

1 (16 oz.) can red, tart pie cherries
2/3 cup sugar
1½ Tbsp. Minute Tapioca
dash of salt
2-3 dashes of cinnamon
1 tsp. lemon juice
2-3 drops almond extract
1½ Tbsp. flour
¼ cup sugar
1 Tbsp. butter, cut into chunks
1-2 tsp. of milk
a recipe for a double pie crust

Mix first 7 ingredients in a saucepan. Heat
on medium while you make the crust. Then mix
flour and sugar and spread evenly over the bottom
of the unbaked crust. Gently spoon pie filling into
crust so as to not disturb sugar mixture on the
bottom. Dot top of filling with butter. Add top crust.
Seal edges all the way around. Brush the top
of the crust with milk, and sprinkle lightly with sugar.

~next page...

Bake at 450° for 5 minutes. Reduce temperature to 400° and bake 25-30 minutes or until golden. Cool on wire rack for 2 hours.

DOUBLE PIE CRUST

2⅓ cups flour
1 tsp. salt

½ cup plus 1 Tbsp. oil
¼ cup plus 1 Tbsp. milk

Mix flour and salt in a bowl. Add oil and milk, stirring until it forms a ball. Divide in half. Wipe counter with a damp cloth and place a piece of plastic wrap on it. Place dough in the middle, cover with another piece of plastic wrap. Roll dough into a circle at least an inch larger than the pie plate. Remove plastic wrap. Sliding hands under bottom piece of plastic wrap, lift dough and turn it over into a pie plate. Roll out remaining dough in similar fashion for the top of your pie. Cut "vents" or design into dough before turning it onto the filling. If preparing a pre-baked crust, prick the crust with a fork thoroughly, across the bottom and around the sides. It is especially important to poke holes with a fork at the juncture of the bottom surface and the sides of crust. Bake for 10-12 minutes at 400°.

Turtle Pie

This ice cream pie was a favorite at our restaurant ~ it is especially wicked and rich.

1 graham cracker pie crust
2 quarts vanilla ice cream
1 cup pecan pieces
1 jar caramel ice cream topping
1 bottle or jar of "Magic Shell" or "Gold Brick" chocolate ~ ice cream topping ~ hot fudge sauce may be substituted ~ here, if desired.

Let ice cream stand at room temperature for 10-15 minutes. Then spoon into graham cracker crust. The ice cream should be high in the center of the pie and meet even with the crust edges on the side. Shaping will be easier if you place a large piece of plastic wrap over the top of the pie, and smooth out gently with your hands until the ice cream is evenly distributed. Put pie into the freezer until firm, about 2-3 hours or longer. Slice into sixths. Garnish each piece with caramel, pecans and chocolate topping. Serve immediately.

Cookies and Brownies

The Best Chocolate Chip COOKIES

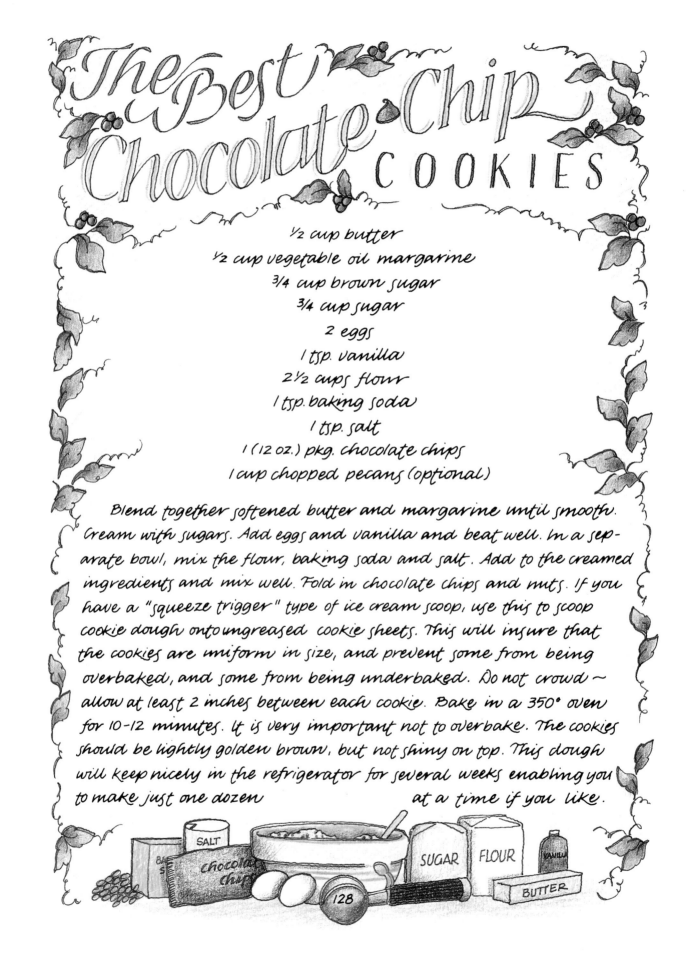

½ cup butter

½ cup vegetable oil margarine

¾ cup brown sugar

¾ cup sugar

2 eggs

1 tsp. vanilla

2½ cups flour

1 tsp. baking soda

1 tsp. salt

1 (12 oz.) pkg. chocolate chips

1 cup chopped pecans (optional)

Blend together softened butter and margarine until smooth. Cream with sugars. Add eggs and vanilla and beat well. In a separate bowl, mix the flour, baking soda and salt. Add to the creamed ingredients and mix well. Fold in chocolate chips and nuts. If you have a "squeeze trigger" type of ice cream scoop, use this to scoop cookie dough onto ungreased cookie sheets. This will insure that the cookies are uniform in size, and prevent some from being overbaked, and some from being underbaked. Do not crowd ~ allow at least 2 inches between each cookie. Bake in a 350° oven for 10-12 minutes. It is very important not to overbake. The cookies should be lightly golden brown, but not shiny on top. This dough will keep nicely in the refrigerator for several weeks enabling you to make just one dozen at a time if you like.

SALT

chocolate chips

SUGAR   FLOUR   VANILLA

BUTTER

Martha's SUGAR·COOKIES

A favorite of everyone who visits Bill and Martha Dahlor's home, these light and crispy sugar cookies are easy to make (no rolling pin required!). They literally "melt in your mouth". (A note from Shelly: Thank you, Martha for all the batches you sent home with me, and for sharing this family recipe with us!)

1 cup butter or margarine	1 cup granulated sugar
1 cup powdered sugar	1 cup cooking oil
2 eggs	1 tsp. vanilla
4 cups, plus 1 Tbsp. flour	1 tsp. salt
1 tsp. cream of tartar	1 tsp. soda

• Cream together butter, granulated and powdered sugars, and oil until light. Add eggs, one at a time, and vanilla. In another bowl, sift together flour, salt, cream of tartar and soda. Add to creamed mixture a little at a time mixing well between additions. Turn mixer to high speed and beat until light and fluffy. Using two teaspoons, spoon out quarter-sized dabs of dough and drop onto an ungreased cookie sheet (use one spoon to scoop dough and the other to push dough off of the other spoon ~ this keeps you from getting your fingers in the dough). Press each lightly with the bottom of a glass that has been dipped in sugar. Bake in a 375° oven for 6-8 minutes or until the sides turn golden brown. Serve with cold milk and enjoy!

Peanut Butter Cookies

This recipe makes a really large batch of cookie dough. The dough keeps in the refrigerator for several weeks, and the cookies freeze very well. Sometimes, I bake half of the dough with chocolate chips added.

18 oz. jar creamy peanut butter

2 cups vegetable oil margarine

2 cups sugar

2 cups brown sugar

4 eggs

2 tsp. vanilla

5 cups flour

4 tsp. baking soda

Cream together peanut butter and margarine. Add sugars, eggs and vanilla. Stir flour and baking soda together in a separate bowl. Add to creamed mixture. Drop by rounded tablespoons onto an ungreased cookie sheet, about 2" apart. Bake at 350° for 10-12 minutes. Do not overbake.

Makes about 6 dozen large cookies.

OATMEAL ♥ COOKIES

1. Cover 1 cup raisins in hot water for 20-30 minutes.

2. Beat together:
- 2 cups shortening
- 2 cups sugar
- 2 cups brown sugar
- 2 tsp. vanilla
- 4 eggs

3. In a separate bowl, mix:
- 3 cups flour
- 2 tsp. baking soda
- 1 tsp. salt

4. Add dry ingredients to creamed ingredients, then add:
- 6 cups rolled oats
- 1 cup chopped pecans (optional)
- raisins from above that have been drained well.

Scoop dough by the heaping tablespoon onto an ungreased cookie sheet about 2" apart. Bake in a 375° oven for 13 to 15 minutes.

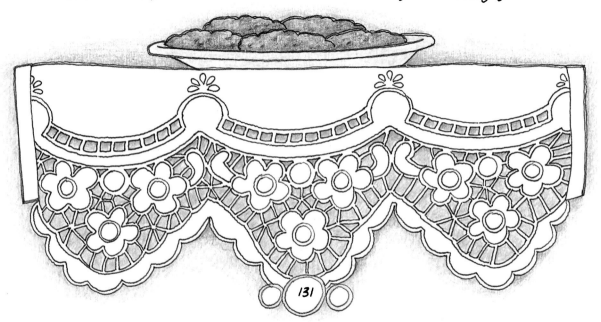

131

SNICKERDOODLES

1 cup vegetable oil margarine
1 ½ cups sugar
2 eggs
2 ¾ cups flour
2 tsp. cream of tartar
1 tsp. baking soda
¼ tsp. salt
3 Tbsp. sugar and 3 tsp. cinnamon, mixed
together in a large shallow bowl
or plate.

Cream together sugar and margarine.
Add eggs and blend well. In a separate bowl,
mix flour, cream of tartar, baking soda, and
salt together. Add to creamed mixture and
mix well. Shape dough in 1" balls and roll
in the cinnamon-sugar mixture. Place 2"
apart on an ungreased cookie sheet. Bake
for 8-10 minutes at 350°
Makes about 5 dozen cookies.

CHOCOLATE Crinkles

When we had our bakery,
these cookies were my son's favorites.
I remember an occasion once, when he was
about 18 months old... I caught him trying to
climb into the bakery case to seize one of them...
...nice try, Blake!

½ cup vegetable oil

4 oz. unsweetened chocolate, melted

2 cups sugar

4 eggs

2 tsp. vanilla

2 cups flour

2 tsp. baking powder

½ tsp. salt

2 cups powdered sugar

🌷 Mix oil, chocolate and sugar. Blend in one
egg at a time until well mixed. Add vanilla. Stir
flour, baking powder and salt into oil mixture. Chill
several hours. Shape into 1" balls. Roll in powdered
sugar. Place 2" apart onto a greased baking sheet.
Bake 10-12 minutes at 350°...
Do not overbake.

Chunky Chocolate and Coconut Cookies

- 2 cups flour
- 1 tsp. salt
- ½ cup butter
- ½ cup sugar
- 1 egg
- 1 tsp. baking soda
- ½ cup margarine
- ¾ cup brown sugar
- 1 tsp. vanilla
- ¼ cup sour cream

Mix flour, baking soda and salt together and set aside. Cream together the margarine, butter, sugars and vanilla. Blend in egg and sour cream. Add dry ingredients to creamed mixture and fold in:

1 cup broken nuts

8 oz. broken chocolate pieces

(use a large chocolate candy bar for this, such as Hershey's or Nestle's)

1 cup shredded coconut

Drop by heaping tablespoon on ungreased baking sheet. Bake at 375° for 10-14 minutes or until light golden brown. Makes about 2-3 dozen.

Sunny's Venice Butter Rounds

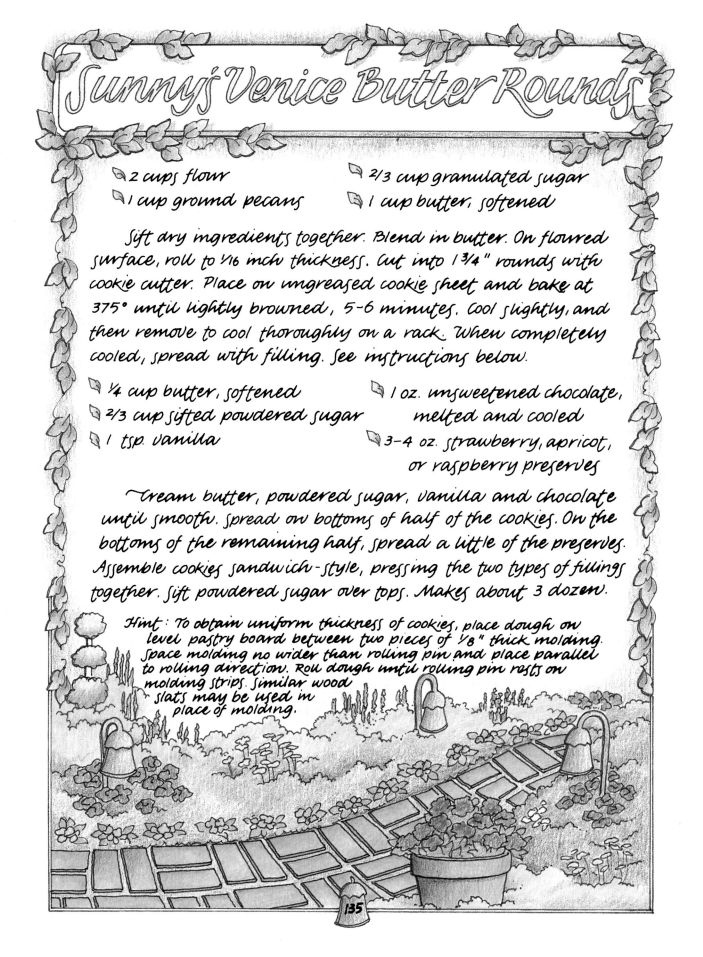

- 2 cups flour
- 1 cup ground pecans
- 2/3 cup granulated sugar
- 1 cup butter, softened

Sift dry ingredients together. Blend in butter. On floured surface, roll to 1/16 inch thickness. Cut into 1¾" rounds with cookie cutter. Place on ungreased cookie sheet and bake at 375° until lightly browned, 5-6 minutes. Cool slightly, and then remove to cool thoroughly on a rack. When completely cooled, spread with filling. See instructions below.

- ¼ cup butter, softened
- 2/3 cup sifted powdered sugar
- 1 tsp. vanilla
- 1 oz. unsweetened chocolate, melted and cooled
- 3-4 oz. strawberry, apricot, or raspberry preserves

Cream butter, powdered sugar, vanilla and chocolate until smooth. Spread on bottoms of half of the cookies. On the bottoms of the remaining half, spread a little of the preserves. Assemble cookies sandwich-style, pressing the two types of fillings together. Sift powdered sugar over tops. Makes about 3 dozen.

Hint: To obtain uniform thickness of cookies, place dough on level pastry board between two pieces of 1/8" thick molding. Space molding no wider than rolling pin and place parallel to rolling direction. Roll dough until rolling pin rests on molding strips. Similar wood slats may be used in place of molding.

No Bake Cookies

2 cups sugar
1/4 cup cocoa
1/2 cup milk
1/2 cup margarine
1/2 tsp. vanilla
pinch of salt
1/2 cup peanut butter
3 cups rolled oats

Mix sugar, cocoa, milk and margarine in a saucepan. Stir over medium heat until it boils. Remove from heat and cool for 1 minute. Then add remaining ingredients and mix well. Drop by teaspoonful onto wax paper. Let cool completely before removing from wax paper.

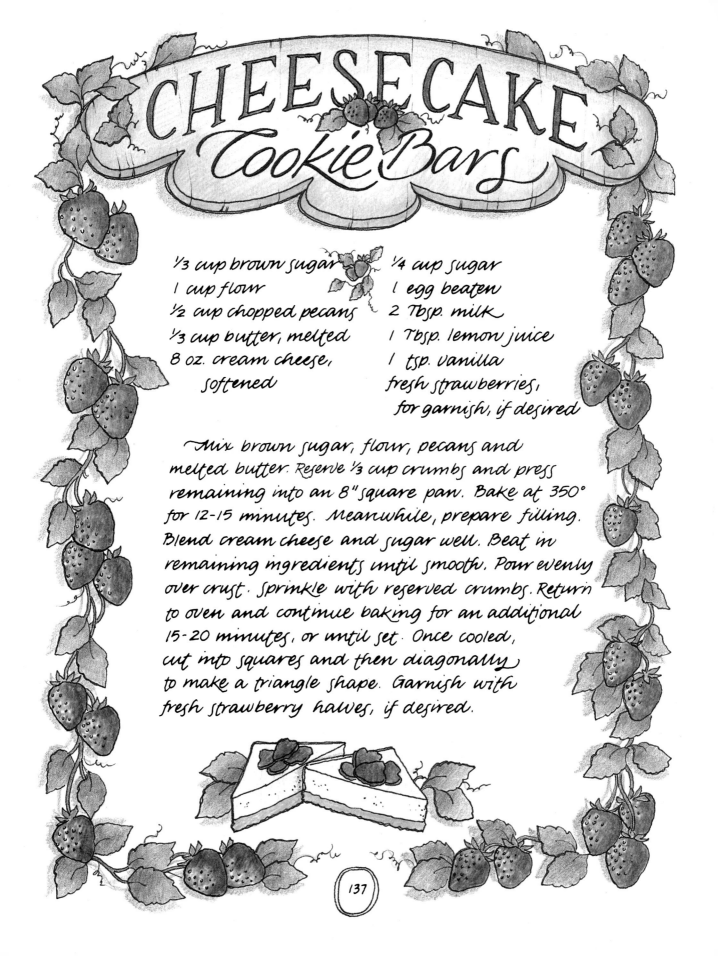

CHEESECAKE Cookie Bars

⅓ cup brown sugar
1 cup flour
½ cup chopped pecans
⅓ cup butter, melted
8 oz. cream cheese,
   softened

¼ cup sugar
1 egg beaten
2 Tbsp. milk
1 Tbsp. lemon juice
1 tsp. vanilla
fresh strawberries,
   for garnish, if desired

Mix brown sugar, flour, pecans and melted butter. Reserve ⅓ cup crumbs and press remaining into an 8" square pan. Bake at 350° for 12-15 minutes. Meanwhile, prepare filling. Blend cream cheese and sugar well. Beat in remaining ingredients until smooth. Pour evenly over crust. Sprinkle with reserved crumbs. Return to oven and continue baking for an additional 15-20 minutes, or until set. Once cooled, cut into squares and then diagonally to make a triangle shape. Garnish with fresh strawberry halves, if desired.

PIZZA COOKIES

- ½ cup butter or margarine
- ¾ cup brown sugar
- 1 egg
- 1 tsp. vanilla
- ¾ cup flour
- dash salt
- ½ tsp. baking powder
- ½ tsp. baking soda
- 1 cup rolled oats
- ½ cup shredded coconut
- 1 cup chocolate chips
- ½ cup chopped pecans
- 1 cup M and M's

Cream together butter and sugar. Add egg and vanilla and beat until smooth. Add flour, salt, baking powder and soda. Mix well. Add oats, coconut, chocolate chips, and pecans. Stir until well blended. Spread cookie dough onto a greased 12" pizza pan to within ½" of the edge of the pan. Sprinkle M and M's evenly over the top. Bake at 350° for 13-15 minutes or until golden brown. Cut into wedges and serve... great for children's birthday parties! Hint: You will probably have close to ½ cup more cookie dough than you will need to make 1 "pizza". Rather than putting all of the dough in the pan (and risk losing some of it over the side as it spreads out in the oven), save the extra and freeze or refrigerate. This dough makes nice "regular size" cookies as well.

Wickerleigh's Tea Bars

Mix in the order listed:

2 eggs
1 cup sugar
1 tsp. vanilla
½ cup butter, melted

Add:

1 cup chopped pecans
½ cup coconut
1 cup chocolate chips

Take 1 <u>unbaked pie crust</u> and press it into the bottom
and sides of a 10" x 7" baking pan. Turn the above mixture
into the pie crust and bake at 350° for 35-40 minutes or
until golden brown. Let cool completely before slicing.
Wonderful with ice cream.

TOFFEE Bars

1 cup butter
1 cup brown sugar
1 egg yolk
2 cups flour
1 tsp. vanilla
6 oz. milk chocolate, broken into small pieces
1 cup chopped pecans

Cream butter and sugar
until light. Mix in egg yolk.
Add flour, stirring just until
blended. Add vanilla. Press
in a 10" x 15" pan. Bake 20-25
minutes at 350°. While still
hot, distribute chocolate on
top and spread gently. Sprinkle
with pecans. Cut while still
warm.
Makes about 2 dozen.

Ann's SQUIRREL Bars

My friend, Ann, has three beautiful daughters. When the girls were small, she used to make Peanut Butter Swirl Bars for them. The youngest (Carrie) had a little bit of trouble pronouncing the word "swirl". Consequently, these cookie bars were renamed "Squirrel Bars." Ann and Doug have moved half a continent away. But they will always be close to my heart...

½ cup peanut butter
⅓ cup butter
3/4 cup brown sugar
3/4 cup sugar

2 eggs, beaten
2 tsp. vanilla
1 cup flour
1 tsp. baking powder

6 oz. chocolate chips

Mix together first four ingredients. Add eggs and vanilla. Stir in flour and baking powder. Spread mixture in a greased 9" x 13" pan. Sprinkle chips on top. Bake 3 minutes at 350°. Take out and "marbelize." Return to oven for another 18-20 minutes. Cool and cut into bars to serve. Serves 8-10.

CARMELITAS

1 cup flour
1 cup oats
3/4 cup brown sugar
1/2 tsp. baking soda
1/4 tsp. salt
3/4 cup butter
12 oz. jar caramel
   ice cream topping
   plus 3 Tbsp. flour

6 oz. chocolate chips
1/2 cup chopped pecans

Mix first six ingredients in a large mixing bowl. Press half of mixture in a 9" x 9" greased baking pan. Bake 10 minutes at 350°. Mix ice cream topping with 3 Tbsp. flour. Spread over oatmeal base and sprinkle with chocolate chips and pecans, then with the rest of the oatmeal mixture. Bake an additional 15-20 minutes. Let cool before cutting. Serves 6-8.

SHORTBREAD
C · O · O · K · I · E · S

This recipe is best when baked in a ceramic pan, designed especially for shortbread. However, you may use a small cake pan if you like.

½ cup lightly salted butter, room temperature
⅓ cup powdered sugar
¼ tsp. vanilla
1 cup flour

Cream the butter until light. Mix in the powdered sugar and vanilla until smooth. Add flour and mix until smooth. Spray the shortbread pan lightly with oil. Press the dough into the pan. Prick the entire surface with a fork. Bake at 325° for 30-35 minutes, or until very lightly browned. Cool in the pan for about 10 minutes. Then loosen the edges with a knife and flip the pan over onto a cutting board. Cut into serving pieces while it is still warm. Dust with powdered sugar, if desired.

Wonderful with fresh fruit.

JAN'S BROWNIES...

This is a wonderful fudge brownie recipe that my sister, Jan, shared with me about ten years ago. Since then some variations of this basic recipe have been created, borrowing some ideas from other favorites. Follow Jan's fudge brownie recipe and then before spreading the batter in the pan, look over the other four options listed under "Etc." on the following page.

1 cup butter or margarine, melted
2 cups sugar
2 tsp. vanilla
4 eggs
2/3 cup cocoa
1 cup flour
½ tsp. baking powder
½ tsp. salt

Cream together the butter and sugar until light. Beat in the vanilla and eggs. Add cocoa, flour, baking powder, and salt and mix well. Turn into a greased 9"x 13" baking pan and bake for 23-25 minutes at 350°. Frost with chocolate icing, or sprinkle with powdered sugar... or try any of the following variations with this basic batter...

....AND ETC.

Fudge-Nut Brownies

Add ½ cup chopped pecans, walnuts, or sliced almonds to the batter before baking.

Mississippi Mud

Add ½ cup flaked coconut to batter. Spread batter in the prepared pan. Bake 18-22 minutes or until toothpick, when inserted in the center, comes out clean. Immediately top with ½ bag of miniature marshmallows. Let cool 5 minutes. Spread marshmallows gently over the top of brownies. Top with ½ cup chopped pecans and this fudge frosting:

¼ cup butter, melted   ½ tsp. vanilla

3 Tbsp. cocoa   3 Tbsp. milk

2 cups powdered sugar
...Mix all together and beat until smooth.

Cream Cheese Brownies

Spread fudge batter in a prepared pan. Prepare one recipe of "Cream Cheese Danish Filling" (from page 35), and drop one tablespoon of filling on top of fudge batter every inch or so. Stick a knife straight down into the batter and draw through both batters, "marbelizing". Bake at 350° for 24 - 28 minutes.

Stolen Heaven

This is a sinful combination of the above variations. Omit the coconut from the Mississippi Mud recipe. Spread the cream cheese filling on top of the fudge batter. Bake at 350° for 25-28 minutes. While still warm, top with marshmallows, nuts and icing. Cool completely before cutting.

Hello Dollies

2 cups graham cracker crumbs
⅓ cup butter, melted
2 cups chocolate chips
1 cup chopped pecans
1 cup shredded coconut
1 can sweetened condensed milk

Preheat oven to 350°. Mix graham cracker crumbs and melted butter. Press in the bottom of a 9" x 13" baking pan. Layer remaining ingredients evenly over the crust. Bake about 20-25 minutes or until coconut is golden brown.

Serves 10-12.

Miscellaneous

" Piece by loving piece, we become whole."
Year by year, we soften with the wear
we are a work of art."

ROXIE'S PUNCH

There is nothing exotic about this punch recipe. We served gallons and gallons of it at the restaurant every day. I think the thing that made it so appealing was the way we presented it: One giant strawberry, an orange and a lemon wedge garnished every sparkling glass. If mint was in season, we threw some of that in for extra measure. It was as fun to look at as it was refreshing. Mix all of the ingredients below together in a large container. Store in the refrigerator until use. Garnish each glass with fresh fruit, or float fruit pieces in the punch bowl.

8 cups cold water
1 cup lemon juice
(fresh or bottled)
♥
1 cup sugar
1 large can frozen orange juice concentrate, undiluted
♥
a few drops red food coloring, if desired until "peachy" in color.

~for~ G·A·R·N·I·S·H

strawberries
lemons
oranges
fresh peaches
fresh pineapple
cherries
etc.
any ♥ or ♥ all

HOT COCOA mix

This would make a great gift for a college-bound student. Fill a giant cannister with this mix, and add 3 to 4 mugs to the package to make it complete . . .

4 pound box non-fat instant milk
2 pound box Nestle's Quick (powdered variety)
1 jar non-dairy creamer
2 cups sugar

Mix and store in a cool dry place. Four heaping teaspoons in a cup of boiling water make one cup of cocoa.

FRIENDSHIP TEA

When we opened the doors of the restaurant in 1981, we decided that it would be fun to offer a selection of teas, of the hot and cold persuasion, to our customers. An occasional customer would look panic-stricken as they raced through the beverage section of the menu, in fear that we would not offer "just regular iced tea". We did, in fact, have the best brewed "regular" tea in the country (in my humble opinion). But for those of you who are a bit more adventurous, try this simple and subtle, flavored iced tea for a change:

Bring 3 cups of water to a boil. Remove from heat. Add to it 1 family-size tea bag (I prefer Lipton Decaffeinated) and 2 small Constant Comment tea bags. Cover the pan with a lid. Steep 5-10 minutes. Pour over ice. Garnish with orange and/or lemon if desired.

PLAY · DOUGH

This recipe is edible, but not tasty...

Mix in a medium-size saucepan:

1 cup flour
¼ cup salt
2 Tbsp. cream of tartar

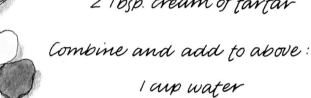

Combine and add to above:

1 cup water
2 tsp. food coloring
1 Tbsp. vegetable oil

Cook over medium heat, stirring constantly for about 5 minutes. When it forms a ball in the center of the pan, turn out and knead on a lightly floured surface. Store in an airtight container or a plastic bag.

Dreams

"If one advances confidently
in the direction of his dreams,
and endeavors to live
the life which he has imagined,
he will meet with a success
unexpected in common hours...
If you have built castles in the air,
your work need not be lost;
that is where they should be.
Now put foundations under them."

~ Henry David Thoreau

"Live decently, fearlessly, joyously ~
and don't forget that in the long run
~ it is not the years in your life
but the life in your years that counts!"

~ Adlai Stevenson

GIFT BASKET
· IDEAS ·
for all ages

BIRTH to ONE YEAR OLD...
"The Bath Basket"

♥ Line a large white, wicker basket with a soft baby bath towel and fill with a bottle of baby bath, shampoo, wash cloths, a comb and brush set, a rubber ducky, powder lotion, a good ointment for diaper rash, and cotton balls. Attach a big bow on the side. Make a tag in the shape of an old claw foot tub and include your best wishes.

ONE to THREE YEARS OLD...
The "One Man Band Basket"

♥ if you can locate an old bushel basket (the type apples used to come in), this would be a perfect start. Fill it with a drum (you may want to make one out of an empty oatmeal box, or purchase a more sophisticated one at the store) a whistle, a harmonica, a tambourine, a xylophone, etc.

THREE to FIVE YEARS OLD
"The Budding Artist Basket"

A bright colored basket would work well for this particular age.

Include any of the following: Crayons, washable markers, coloring books, "paint with water" books, water color paints and brushes, safety scissors, and a few containers of play dough (there is a recipe for play dough in this book!), with cookie cutters. Make an artist's palette for the tag.

❤

FIVE to SEVEN YEARS OLD...
"The Backpack Basket"

These items may be put in a backback for the child, or the backpack and all of the items may be put in a box or a basket: Bookplates, with the child's name engraved on them (these may be purchased at most stationery stores), pencil box, three or four books suited for this age, a ruler, pencil sharpener, and last-but-not-least, a wallet with the child's own library card in it. You might include a note with the promise of a trip to the local library within a few days.

❤

SEVEN to TEN YEARS OLD...
"The Desk and Doodle Basket"

Fill with his or her very own personal set of desk accessories or craft "tools". You might include items like a nice pair of scissors in a neon or pastel color, a stapler, a Scotch tape dispenser, a ruler, pencil sharpener, some engraved stationery and stamps. Or a nice tool box could be filled with a screwdriver, a hammer, a tape measure, a ruler, a block of wood, nails, pliers, etc.

TEN to TWELVE YEARS OLD...

This is perhaps the most difficult age to please in gift-giving. They are not yet young adults. But they definitely do not consider themselves children. It seems best to try and concentrate on a hobby or special interest, and make that your theme. For example:

"The Beach Basket"
sun-screen, a beach towel, large-toothed comb, a teen magazine, a deck of playing cards, sunglasses, etc.

or

"The Baking Basket"
a cookbook, some measuring cups and spoons, a rolling pin, some spatulas, cookie cutters, hot pads, etc.

"The Nature's Friend Basket"
a bug catcher, books on endangered species, a cricket box, binoculars, bird seed, a compass, bug repellant, a canteen, etc.

or

"The Good Sport Basket"
baseball cards and album, tickets to a game, sporting equipment, etc.

TWELVE to FIFTEEN YEARS OLD...
"The Bottomless Pit Basket"

Fill with snack foods of all varieties, gift certificates to local fast food chains or ice cream shops, a roll of quarters for vending machine emergencies.

FIFTEEN to SEVENTEEN YEARS OLD...
"Driving You Crazy Basket"

Make a tag to resemble a license plate, and include inside: the keys to the car, a key chain, car wax, a chamois, a contract stating under which conditions the car may be driven, with blank lines for you and the young driver to agree upon and fill out, stating what will happen if the rules are broken, and a business size card on which you will write of your unconditional love for them. This card should be carried with them right alongside their driver's license.

EIGHTEEN to TWENTY ONE YEARS OLD...
"You're on Your Own Basket"

A mending kit, an address book, a dozen stamped envelopes all addressed to Mom and/or Dad, quarters for laundry, coupons, a Bible, family recipes, etc.

ANY AGE ADULT...

Again, it's best to find a theme that surrounds a particular interest or hobby. Food is always a welcome sight at any age. Perhaps a specific type of food or beverage that you know this person loves could be the central idea. You could also concentrate on their chosen profession as a theme. For instance, a teacher might enjoy a...

"Teacher's Pet Basket"

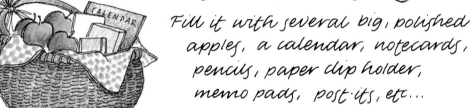

Fill it with several big, polished apples, a calendar, notecards, pencils, paper clip holder, memo pads, post-its, etc...

SENIOR ADULT...

"The Best is Yet to Be Basket"

... an assortment of greeting cards and a card organizer that lists special dates involving friends and family members, fresh fruit, gift certificate for favorite restaurant, a miniature purse-size photo album with all of the children and grandchildren pictured and a short message written by each one of them, a deck of playing cards, theatre tickets.

"Life is a succession of moments.
To live each one is to succeed."
~ Corita Kent ~

Index